I Do. I Did.
Now What?!

I Do. I Did. Now What?!

Life After the Wedding Dress

by Jenny Lee

WORKMAN PUBLISHING • NEW YORK

DEDICATION

For the love of my life, my darling
husband, Cosmas, who inspires not only
my sense of humor, but also my heart.

Library of Congress Cataloging-in-Publication Data
Lee, Jenny.
Ido. I did. Now what? : life after the wedding dress / Jenny Lee.
p. cm.
ISBN 0-7611-2599-X
1. Marriage. 2. Interpersonal relations. I. Title.
HQ734 .L3775 2003

306.81—dc21   2002069015

Workman books are available at special discounts when purchased in bulk for
premiums and sales promotions as well as for fund-raising or educational use.
Special editions or book excerpts can also be created to specification.
For details, contact the Special Sales Director at the address below.

Design by Janet Vicario

WORKMAN PUBLISHING COMPANY, INC.
708 Broadway
New York, NY 10003-9555
www.workman.com

Printed in the U.S.A.
First printing January 2003

10 9 8 7 6 5 4 3 2 1

CONTENTS

INTRODUCTION • VI

I Do. I Did. Now What?!

FOREWORD • XI

Life Before the Dress

CHAPTER ONE • I

From This Day Forward

CHAPTER TWO • 37

To Have and to Hold

CHAPTER THREE • 80

For Richer or Poorer

CHAPTER FOUR • 110

In Sickness and Health

CHAPTER FIVE • 144

For Better or Worse

CHAPTER SIX • 190

To Love, Honor, and Cherish

CHAPTER SEVEN • 231

Until Death Do Us Part

Introduction

I Do. I Did. Now What?!

When I first got engaged, all I did was stare at my new diamond ring. Ooooh, look how shiny it is. Ooooh, look how it sparkles. Doesn't it look nice as I'm typing on my keyboard; doesn't it look nice as I'm walking down the street; doesn't it look nice with everything I own; and wouldn't it look even nicer with a new handbag, skirt, or pair of Jimmy Choo shoes? This new diamond ring had become a symbol of the promise of a whole new shiny life—marriage. But let's talk about the other defining characteristic of a diamond: the fact that it can cut through glass. Because as shiny and fabulous as marriage often is, it can also be hard as hell.

I was wholly unprepared for how big an impact marriage would have on my life. Sure I was into the whole "wedding" thing—all my friends in one room, the fabulous Vera Wang dress that makes me feel like a queen, and, of course, the cake. I mean, who doesn't like a good party where she's the guest of honor and everyone can't help but smile and fawn. I felt as if I'd won a beauty contest or something. But what I'm talking about is the aftermath, the stillness after the storm, when you peek out to see if your mailbox is still standing—after the room service of club sandwiches and French fries (I hadn't eaten in months); after the five-hundred-dollar silk negligee is lying on the floor, having made its all-too-brief appearance (I think I wore the damn thing for like three minutes tops); and after he's fallen asleep, when you find yourself in the dark thinking, I'm married. Now what?

It's just that no one clues you in ahead of time about everything that's involved. Sure, your mom has told you plenty, but over the years you've learned to dismiss her advice almost automatically—she's practically a Flintstone as far as you're concerned. Like you're really going to spend your weekends ironing and making casseroles. I certainly tried to get some inkling from my few married friends of what was to come after the "I do"s, but they'd just shrug, then emphatically pronounce that my wedding day would be one of the best days of my life. Next, their eyes starry, they would begin to tell me about their own wedding, speaking in a strange, hushed tone; I'd interrupt them and say, "Yes, I remember; I was there—it was certainly magical, and you looked really really thin—but c'mon, tell me about after the wedding. What's life like *after* the dress? What is it like to be a wife?"

This is when I'd get some vague answer about it being "an adjustment, but overall it's really nice," and then they'd switch the subject, wanting to talk about *the* wedding dress and all the trimmings—long veil or short, headpiece or tiara, French bustle or American style. But I didn't want to talk about the dress, well, not right that second. What does that mean . . . "adjustment"? Isn't that what you get from a chiropractor? "Nice"? What the hell is that supposed to mean?

I half imagined there might be some secret marriage pact that says you can't share the mysteries of marriage with the world of the single. But what's the big secret? The suspense kept me up nights for a while, but eventually I chalked it up to my not having had chocolate for weeks (in hopes of having skinny arms for my wedding photos). I figured I just had a little prewedding paranoia, right? In fact, maybe the reason no one could tell me the real deal about marriage is because it's so utterly amazing they don't even know where to start. Now we're talking.

Well, what it came down to is that I had absolutely no clue what to expect from marriage. I'm not saying that was necessarily a bad thing, but I will say that I wish I had seen the sign that said BUCKLE UP, WILD RIDE AHEAD. The beginning of a marriage is a roller coaster of huge life changes, and we all know what that means— major emotional loop de loops.

So you get married, and you're incredibly happy. The honeymoon is a blast (in case you didn't know, honeymoon calories don't count!), and when you get back, you're still totally euphoric, even though you have to go back to work. You move in together (unless you're already shacked up), and then you wake up one morning, walk into the kitchen, and suddenly you're like, "What have I done? Why did I get married? WHO ON EARTH WOULD LEAVE A MUSTARD-COVERED KNIFE ON A CLEAN KITCHEN TOWEL, AND HOW COULD I BE LEGALLY BOUND TO SUCH A MAN?" (See Chapter 2 for full details.) Then you think, Who cares if I have to give back all my presents? (C'mon, does a woman who lived out her entire twenty-something existence with nothing in the fridge but Diet Coke really need a ten-piece All-Clad cookware set?) And, of course, you wonder how long it would take your mother to track you down and kill you after you flee the country. But you get over it and remember that he automatically wraps his arms around you whenever you draw close to him in bed (even when he's asleep), that he

I was wholly unprepared for how big an impact marriage would have on my life.

sacrifices his own belly warmth by letting you put your cold hands under his shirt whenever they're cold, that you've got a date every Friday night for eternity, and that his face breaks into a smile that says he's happy to be home when he comes through the door and sees you sitting there.

So fine, your emotions fluctuate a bit; we all deal with that every month. After a while you realize that a lot of things that seemed like very big deals at the time are not so big when you think of them relative to the next sixty years of your life. What's one kitchen towel in the grand scheme of things if you never again have to take out the trash? I mean, when you think about marriage and all that goes with it (the in-laws, the mortgage, your married friends, the fact that you can't ever get him to fill up the Brita water pitcher), it can seem terribly complicated. But at its very core it's almost laughably and profoundly simple. The four things that you need are love (because there will be a day when you catch him using your expensive shampoo), effort (walking to the video store is not considered a night out on the town), time (keep in mind that you'll never ever be able to do everything on your to-do list, so you might as well have some fun together because, trust me, the laundry will still be there tomorrow), and, most important (well, in *my* humble opinion) a sense of humor (if you look hard enough, you can find laughter in almost any situation).

In some ways marriage is everything I've ever wanted (someone to kill the spiders and change the lightbulbs). But it's not quite the glass-slipper fantasy—you know, where you marry the prince, live in a castle, throw fabulous parties, and buy shoes all the time. Married life contains an inordinate amount of everyday challenges with which you have to learn to deal, and the responsibilities are forever—till death do you part. But then . . . you can be surprised. One night when you're very cranky, and all the shows are repeats, and you've already read all the fashion mags for the month, and you're in the bedroom trying on your old party shoes thinking that your feet are all dressed up with no place to go—your husband, your prince, will suddenly appear by your side . . . and present you with a grilled cheese sandwich that he's made just for you.

In some ways marriage is everything I've ever wanted (someone to kill the spiders and change the lightbulbs).

Foreword

LIFE BEFORE THE DRESS

I met my husband five years ago when we were both living in Manhattan, and I can honestly say that I thought about marriage on our very first date. (I can also say that my husband did not think about marriage once during our first date, but he did think that I looked skinny, which is close enough.) Don't start to think, however, that I'm getting all weepy and mushy on you and saying that it was love at first sight (he had long hair, so that was out)—that I knew during dinner he was the man I would marry—because that's not true; it would be several hours before I figured it out. I guarantee that if you were to ask most single women who have started to consider settling down, they could think about marriage, or something related to it—living together, having children, shopping for real estate, etc.—at least fifty times during the first date alone. It's what we do.

During our first date I asked Cosmas to tell me about his work in medicine and research, which he did, but it was way beyond A.P. chemistry, so I started to space out. To make sure I looked as if I was still paying attention and was utterly fascinated by everything he was saying, I used the trick I always use in this situation—I stared at part of his face. I always used to choose the nose, but you have to be careful; if you stare at it too long and with too much verve, you end up going a bit cross-eyed, which on a date is not the best look. This time I chose the eyes.

It was then that I noticed he had the longest eyelashes I had ever seen (well, without mascara), that weren't fake, and that were on a man. They were soooo long. Such a waste on a guy; I knew women who would kill for such lashes—thick, silky, and curled up just perfectly. How darling. My own eyelashes were a disaster—short, straight, and pointing down instead of curling up—hopeless. It occurred to me that if I married a guy with fabulous eyelashes, then my future daughters had a chance to inherit them. And that's where it began—as next I tried to decide what our kids would look like. Cosmas's hair was sort of wavy; would they have wavy hair? Wavy hair sucks in humidity; we would have to live somewhere dry. Would they be smart? What if my English major tendencies totally canceled out all of his brainiac science stuff, then what? But would it be such a bad thing? Would they be popular? Would they get mercilessly teased due to his incredibly long Greek last name? Would I change my name? (Mentally I write in cursive "Mrs. Jenny Lee Giallourakis.") Would I use the correct cursive *G* or would I use a script *G* with a fancy tail connecting it? Ooooh, that would be nice. Where would we live? Perhaps in the West where it's dry (because of the hair). I've always liked Mediterranean-style houses: white stone, red-tile roof. But if I married a Greek guy and lived in one of those houses, would that be cheesy, like we were trying to build our own little Santorini in Scottsdale? Would his last name even fit on our mailbox? What font would

I use when they stenciled our name on our mailbox? Something reminiscent of calligraphy, perhaps, but not too swirly.

I saw him take a sip of his drink, which surely meant that he had finished with work talk, and I smiled real big; I now had in my head the perfect image of our mailbox (black, shiny but with texture, silver lettering in 26-point type, a nice Garamond font—no, not Garamond, a nice Monotype Corsiva font; and instead of a plain red flag, perhaps a mini-American flag? I know, we could design our own family flag!), and I said, without missing a beat, "Your work sounds absolutely fascinating! Really, really interesting. I guess I should have paid more attention in chemistry. Who knew?"

By the end of the first date, which neither of us wanted to end (superb dinner, awesome conversation, our eyes and lips locked from eleven P.M. on.), we got kicked out of the coffee shop at two A.M. He hailed me a cab and gave me my last kiss of the evening. I walked a few steps toward the waiting cab, and, even though I know you're never supposed to turn around for the last look, I couldn't help myself. I just had to see him one more time. So I turned, and he was right behind me holding my elbow, and he said in a soft voice "I didn't want you to slip on the ice," and suddenly I was light-headed, OH MY GOD, HE'S THE ONE. THE SWEETEST GUY IN THE WORLD. HE DIDN'T WANT ME TO SLIP ON THE ICE! CAN YOU BELIEVE THAT? I DIDN'T EVEN KNOW THAT THERE WAS ICE ON THE GROUND, BECAUSE I THOUGHT I WAS FLOATING, FOR GOD'S SAKE! I knew I loved him right then and there.

On our first Valentine's Day he gave me an exquisite, stunning piece of antique jewelry, something I never would have thought to pick out for myself. Now, years later, every time I wear it people still exclaim over it (and are astonished when I say that my husband—a MAN—was able to pick it out himself. "No, he's not gay," I say, answering their silent thoughts). And only months into our romance did I suddenly understand that whenever I received flowers (like, all the time), he was going to the florist to pick them out himself (no, really, he's not gay).

Weekends back then were not about picking up dry cleaning, going to the grocery store, checking the chore list on the refrigerator. No, those weekends were all-out lovefests.

When I think about how totally crazy happy we were together (I nicknamed our love affair *NY Post* Love: it was so intense that one, if not both of us, was bound to end up on the front page—dead or missing) and how much money we spent on cabs going back and forth in the middle of the night . . . I can't help but crack an enormous grin. C'mon, you know the drill, we've all lived it . . . think back to one of those typical evenings when it was almost one A.M. He has a huge exam that he needs to study for, and you should be prepping for a big meeting you have scheduled for the next day; instead, you're on the phone having the same conversation that every couple has when they are falling in love. You're both saying that you miss each other desperately even though you saw each other a few hours ago. Then you go back and forth for a while about what you'd do to each other if you were together (this could go on for a while). Finally, I'd offer the voice of reason; sighing, I would review aloud the reasons we weren't together at that very moment: it was late, we both had to get up early, and we both had stuff we still needed to do for the next day. He'd agree that we needed to get off the phone. I'd agree with him. Then he'd offer to pay for my cab.

And whammo, I was shoving my nicely pressed suit and high heels into a grocery bag, grabbing my lipstick, reaching for the wrong work folder, and flying out the door into the dark of night. Hailing a cab, I'd speed across town, applying lipstick and eyeliner in a dark, moving car like a pro, and I would be deliriously happy. There was no room for reason, practical thought, or the minutiae of everyday life, because my entire body was filled with pulsating, crazy love.

Weekends back then were not about picking up dry cleaning, going to the grocery store, checking the chore list on the refrigerator. No, those weekends were all-out lovefests—kissing for hours, thinking of all the words that begin with the letter L, and reinventing the entire Kama Sutra. Brunch in New York City ends around four P.M, and most weekends we were tearing ourselves out of bed at three-forty, throwing clothes on in a frenzy and making a mad dash to any restaurant that would feed two starving, lovesick people.

So, long story short, after the normal amount of breakups, makeups, and declarations of undying love—he proposed. I said yes, and we went back to my apartment and made French fries (seriously, no euphemism here; all the excitement made us both hungry). Yes, we had a modern fairy-tale romance, but our story continued; a year later we married, and that's where *this* story begins.

CHAPTER ONE

From This
Day Forward

ONCE UPON MY MARRIAGE

My husband told me he selected St. Lucia for our honeymoon destination because it would be romantic, beautiful, and there would be no shopping whatsoever. I told him that although he was the cutest man alive, he was also clearly delusional; in this age of consumerism, there's *always* somewhere to shop—particularly in countries that subsist on the tourist trade. Well, I gotta say, where we were staying, there truly was *no shopping whatsoever*.

The resort had two sad little gift shops, and I visited them both every day in hopes of new shipments of something to buy. My mainstay became those Cadbury Fruit and Nut bars (to eat on the beach and to freeze in our private villa's fridge). They ran out of them on day four, so I was left standing there like an idiot New Yorker, questioning the woman. "What do you mean you're out? When are you getting more in? Should I come back this afternoon?," figuring I could wait a few hours. She shrugged. I took it to the next level. "Can I speak to the manager of the shop?" Blank stare. "Your supervisor?" It turned out she owned the shop and really doesn't keep track of when she gets things. But then again, what could I expect from a store whose total magazine selection consisted of a two-week-old *Time* magazine and a two-month-old *Good Housekeeping*. I was getting a little desperate for media news . . . but not that desperate.

As my withdrawal for all things urban started to wane, and I found something new into which to channel my competitiveness . . . getting up at the crack of dawn and walking down to the private beach, nestled between the Piton Mountains, to claim one of the eight big straw umbrellas. Well, not just any of them, but the one that I wanted, the one I had deemed to be the best—you know, best view, farthest from the kids, away from the public route to the bathroom and snack bar. My umbrella (oops, *our* umbrella—cut me some slack, I had been married like only one hundred plus hours at the time) was a little off center but had a view of everything, and everyone had a view of us—but without our looking as if we wanted to be dead center. It took me four days of getting up earlier and earlier to secure *our* umbrella—but I'm pleased to report that by getting up at five-fifteen A.M. I managed to secure it for the last five days of our vacation. Neurotic tendencies win the day!

Two days before we had to leave, I was really beginning to relax, and I had even considered taking off my watch (I never actually did, but the fact that I would even think about it is a *big* deal). We ate on the beach, ordered room service, hung out on the beach under our great umbrella, played in the pool, went for drinks at the various resort bars, etc. And then, when everything had been going so well, he asked, *the question.*

"I heard they have games at the front desk. Wanna play Scrabble?" Suddenly I felt as though I were on top of a ledge, and everything was terribly precarious because, of course, I wanted to play, I love games, and Scrabble especially. *But,* I do have this tendency to be ridiculously competitive, taking most games far too seriously. I'm an extremist . . . meaning I can either be super-mellow (after about five days of chanting myself into a semi-state of relaxation) or totally hard-core—there was no middle ground.

Of course he knew me and had witnessed my ruthless game playing firsthand . . . (shrieking and jumping up and down on the sofa, screaming how I'm the supreme

4

champion of the world, that kind of thing), so he knew what he was getting himself into, right? Still, the thought of breaking our stretch of perfect warm and fuzzy love made me a little nervous. But, it's not as if we can avoid every potential dicey situation for the rest of our married life. So I said, "Sure, let's play."

And, of course, I was totally kicking his butt. It was the very end of the game, and we both had only a few tiles left. He was taking forever, hoping to dump his high-scoring Q (I'd calculated what letters he had left), and I was taunting him, offering to loan him a U if he'd give me 60 percent of the point score for his word. I mean, it's all in good fun, right? And then, out of nowhere . . . like in a John Woo movie, with pigeons flying off into a dark

And then, when everything had been going so well, he asked, the question.

alleyway . . . his hand moved across the board and he put down his letters, using a U that was already on the board (I had wrongly assumed that every U was virtually locked down due to the surrounding letters) and spelling out Q-U-I-R-K-Y. He received forty-four points and won the game.

I was completely dumbfounded, not to mention somewhat impressed, and, not knowing how to react, I jumped out of my chair and made a run to the bathroom. There I was in the bathroom, staring at my tan, checking my bikini lines, and, as I applied some lipstick, I gave myself a little lecture. "Don't be a sore loser. So you lose one lousy game, big fat deal. It's not the end of the world. Obviously it was some freakish occurrence (basically an X File) because you always, *always* beat him." This was doing nothing for me however, so I tried a new line of reasoning, "This is your honeymoon. He is your husband; you are married to him; you are life partners; you should share in each other's triumphs. In fact, you should be happy that he won, because from now on when he wins, so do you. You're a team, which means you actually haven't really lost at all."

This sorta worked for me, and I managed a tight smile as I marched out of the bathroom and headed back to the table. So I hugged him from behind, kissed him on the neck, and whispered, "Congratulations, honey, that was a great game. You actually beat me." So then he pulled away and said in this totally cocky tone, "Geez, you know I did practically get an eight hundred on my verbal SATs; so it's really not that surprising that I beat you." Rage overtook me like a flash flood. He had basically ignored my grand gesture of love and good faith in even congratulating him at all. He was lucky I hadn't just flipped the board over and let all the tiles go crashing to the stone floor (believe me, I was tempted). So I said, "You are such a jerk." And with that I made a turn of the heel and headed toward the pool.

We were officially having our first married fight.

I settled into a chaise lounge twenty feet away and grumbled under my breath, calculating the final score (he beat me by two little points), and he just stayed put, slowly and meticulously putting away the pieces of the game. Ten minutes passed, and then five more. I had been lying on my back, and now I flipped myself over to stare at the pool. I kept replaying the situation. What went wrong? Maybe my tone was sort of bitchy when I congratulated him. Maybe his point was valid that he does actually have a decent vocabulary, so it wasn't totally unreasonable that he would

We were officially having our first married fight.

win from time to time. At least the fight itself hadn't been a doozy, but it was a little unsettling. I thought about how some small fights can snowball to the point where all hell breaks loose. I pictured us in a tenement throwing pots at each other and screaming, and cops arriving to surround the building. Next the FBI swat team would call in snipers, while a baby (not ours, of course) cried in the background . . . obviously, I'd been watching too much *Law and Order.*

What was odd was that I was no longer single and he was no longer JUST my boyfriend, so the fear of this tiny little fight turning into the breakup scene in a TV show seemed suddenly a moot issue. We were married. There was no quick out, and, of course, I didn't want there to be. Wasn't that the nature of a true commitment anyway? The fact that there was no easy out? I remembered how peaceful I'd been after he finally proposed to me . . . how all those stupid fears and worries had just lifted from my shoulders—all the looming so-where-is-this-relation-ship-going questions finally gone. Instantly, I knew exactly where the relationship was headed . . . down the aisle with me in a Vera Wang dress.

I reviewed the facts in my head. He beat me in Scrabble (barely); I offered him what I thought was a big sincere effort of congrats; he then felt that I was patron-izing him and retaliated by being a jerk. But the real deal here was that this fight had absolutely no relevance to the big picture of our lives. Obviously we weren't going to *break up* over a Scrabble game, and in fact I couldn't even *threaten* to break up. If we'd been characters in a sitcom, I suppose one of us could have ended up on the couch, but this was our honeymoon. Furthermore, this vacation was costing a fortune, and it would be totally stupid of us to waste any of our precious Caribbean time by being annoyed at each other. So, really, there was no point in letting this fight go on any longer than it had to.

Wow. Who knew I could be so practical? It truly was a *major* revelation (either that, or I was starting to get sunstroke), so next I started to wonder whether we would ever fight again, now that I had figured out the whole fighting-when-married thing. Why would we bother if there was no point? (Definitely sunstroke.) So I decided to go make up.

I went and sat back down across from him and apologized without saying the words *I'm sorry*. And he apologized back saying the actual words *I'm sorry*. Which of course made me so damn happy because I hated having to say it first, so then I followed up with "I'm sorry, too." I leaned forward, and we kissed across the table. Then I started to tell him all about my profound new realization. And when I finished, I sat back and asked, "So what were you thinking about?" and he said, "Whether I should order another hot dog now, or whether I should go into the ocean first. Because if I ate the hot dog now, then I'd have to wait thirty minutes before going into the water . . ."

This was the perfect doorway into an entirely new tiff, of course, with me pouting because he obviously hadn't been even remotely fazed by our first "married fight," but I kept my quivering bottom lip in check and let it go. I convinced him to order another hot dog right then, suggesting that we'd both go into the water later, which would give us more than enough time (twenty minutes to get the hot dog, two minutes to eat it, and then thirty minutes to digest on dry land) to play one more game of Scrabble. . . .

I *trounced* him by eighty-nine points.

WIFE STRIFE

While engaged, I never gave a thought to what sort of wife I'd like to be or what marriage really meant to me. I did, however, spend an inordinate amount of time thinking about my wedding dress, my wedding shoes, my hair, my wedding dress, the wedding cake, DJ vs. band, my dress (I was really into the dress), and what sort of wedding ring would look best with my lovely engagement ring. I attributed my behavior to the spell of the sparkly, a state of mind (or rather the state of being out of one's mind) that took over engaged women, when they could think of nothing else except the wedding. It was as if all the hours spent staring at our engagement ring—like all the time (I once walked into a mailbox)—hypnotized us, so it wasn't really our fault.

Due to this one-track wedding mind-set, I was unprepared for the big picture issues of identity that marriage would soon bring up. Looking back, I wondered how it could be possible that I was so naive to think marriage wouldn't be a big deal. I guess I thought I'd still be Jenny—just Jenny with diamonds.

By the time I got engaged and then married a year later, I was in the tail end of my twenties, and it was probably safe to assume that my identity was fairly well formed by then. I believed it was true that women normally defined themselves by their relationships with others, and I was very comfortable with my role as the wanna-be rebel youngest child who dutifully called her mother every Sunday, as the little sister who looked up to her big brother but had to loan him money since he was always broke, as the wild, outrageous anything-goes super-gossipy, but-would-give-you-a-kidney sort of friend, as a manager who believed in team work and would always stay late, as the easygoing, fun girlfriend who was always up for anything, and, of course, one of my favorite roles—as a cool New Yorker.

I was so naive to think marriage wouldn't be a big deal. I guess I thought I'd still be Jenny—just Jenny with diamonds.

Once I was a bridesmaid in a very California wedding, and at one of the cocktail parties preceding the event I found myself chatting up some men at the bar. I was laughing loudly and doing my famously perfected coy move of turning away from my admirers to scan the rest of the crowd as if to say, "I'm a little bored; you must work harder to entertain me. I'm a woman who likes to keep her options open. And, oh, by the way, check out my long dark hair." (Men apparently love long hair.) I noticed that I was the only woman in the room wearing a little black dress, smoking, and flirting. Later that evening I overheard someone ask about me, as I was highly visible amid the sea of pastel colors and blonde highlights, and the other person responded "Oh, she's the bridesmaid from New York." Yep, I loved my role as a sexy, single New York woman, and I was good at it.

I had worked to perfect my role as a swinging single-ton for years. So it didn't seem quite fair to me that after a thirty-minute ceremony, a four-hour '80s dance party (my reception), and a ten-day honeymoon, I suddenly had to play the starring role of wife. It wasn't just that I hadn't had any rehearsal; I hadn't even seen the script! The only things I knew for sure were that I was no longer single (ah, well, it was fun while it lasted), that I was soon to be no longer a New Yorker (we were moving to Boston), and that I was now in need of a new persona.

I just didn't know how this wife thing worked, and I was loath to admit it and too proud to ask. So I started looking around to see how other people were doing it. If I could learn to put my hair in a double French twist sweep by watching an infomercial then surely I could nail this wife thing down in a few weeks.

Unfortunately, I was the first of my close friends to get married, proving that the one you expect to go last, if at all, is always the one who goes first. (It's the same phenomenon as when your friend is desperate to find a pair of shoes for some function and you go shopping with her just for moral support and she can't find what she's looking for but you find and buy two pairs that you don't really need.) The next obvious role model was my mother; she had been married for more than twenty-five years, so surely she knew how to be a wife. But there was a problem, because, no offense to my mom—she's fab and I love her—but when she was a newlywed, wearing green eye shadow and throwing potluck dinners were all the rage. Besides, there was no way that I wanted to be the kind of wife she'd been. She was one of those housewives who did everything for her husband, fixed every meal for him, raised three children, and cleaned the house without any help (translation: slave). It wasn't as if I was never going to cook any of his meals, raise our kids, or clean the house—in fact, I was happy to do all of these things, as long as I wasn't doing them alone.

No way was I going to follow in her footsteps. In fact, I pretty much wanted to have the exact opposite, which is when I came up with the idea of the "anti-wife." So, in order to be a proper anti-wife, I decided I just had to figure out everything I didn't want to be as a wife and then do the opposite. I did not want to become my husband's second mother. I did not want to be the wife who let herself go, gaining weight and not caring about her looks anymore. I did not want to be the wife who let her husband make all the decisions. I did not want to be the wife who always complained about her husband and seemed disgruntled. I did not want to be

How did this happen? Who was crazy enough to let me become a wife?

the wife whose entire life was her husband. I did not want to be the wife who cooked and cleaned all day. Sure, being the anti-wife sounded good on paper, but would it work in reality?

I had no idea if I worried about being a wife more than most other women; as it wasn't one of those things I could easily bring up in conversation. "Raise your hand if the thought of marriage gives you heart-pounding anxiety attacks!" The funny thing was that I felt as if I was having the stereotypical male reaction to the whole thing. With sweaty palms, dry mouth, and a racing heart, I'd say to myself, "I'm married. I'm a married woman. I'm a married woman with a husband." It just didn't sound real to me. Sometimes I'd say it out loud, hoping that by doing so it would feel more real, "Hi. My name is Jenny, and I'm a wife. Hello. So nice to meet you. Yes, yes I'm here with my husband; that's him over there—the cute one—yep, he's my husband, which makes me his wife." Then I'd sort of laugh to myself and think, How did this happen? Who was crazy enough to let me become a wife? Of course it didn't help that all my friends were still in a state of disbelief themselves, shaking their head in wonderment, saying, "It's so hard to think of you married." "I can't believe that you're actually married." "Who would have ever thought that Jenny Lee would up and get married?" It was enough to give a girl a complex about the whole thing.

And to make matters even more surreal, we moved to Boston. We had to because Cosmas had one of those amazing opportunities that he couldn't really turn down, and we made our first husband-wife deal, which was that at the end of his five-year fellowship in Boston I would be the one to choose whether we stayed (doubt it), returned to New York City (probably), or moved anywhere else, for that matter (who knows?). As much as it broke my heart to leave New York, I couldn't help but speculate that it might actually be easier starting off in a whole new place where no one had ever known me as the "girl least likely to get married" and where people would automatically see me and accept me as the average, exceptionally cool married woman.

I was using the exact same Jenny-logic in my transformation from a smoker to a nonsmoker. I had promised to quit smoking when I got married (a moment of weakness on my part, dammit, but diamonds make you do the dumbest things), and I managed to beg a mini-extension of the nasty habit until we moved. I explained to Cosmas that smoking was an integral part of my whole cool New Yorker personality, and it wasn't as if I could just flip a switch and suddenly be different. There were a few bars where I would go at which the bartender would automatically get me a Diet Coke with lime, slide over an ashtray, and then be ready with a light moments after I sat down. How could I fight against that? I promised him that it would be a completely different scene in Boston. I certainly didn't associate Boston with smoking, and I wasn't known at any of the Boston bars as a smoker, or as anything else. So once we moved, I would just be another random nonsmoking married woman . . . sounded plausible, don'tcha think?

THE FIRST SOCIAL OUTING WE ATTENDED as man and (nonsmoking) wife was for Cosmas's new job. When I read the invitation, I was dismayed to learn that it was a clambake, my first. So not only was this my first time onstage as a wife, it was going to be in a setting with which I was completely unfamiliar; it might as well have been an invitation to walk over hot coals. I started calling my friends, trying to figure out what one wore to a clambake, what happened at a clambake, and what one should bring to a clambake.

I now know that one does not wear an ecru silk spaghetti strap Armani slip dress with a flowing lavender silk scarf and high-heeled sling-back sandals. For some reason, I had this very romantic Gatsby-esque picture in my head of a raging bonfire on a beautiful beach with good-looking Ralph Lauren—type waiters in tuxedos (with their pants rolled up) serving champagne and clams on silver trays. In reality, it was a large white tent set up in a huge front yard in a very affluent neighborhood in the suburbs of Massachusetts with people wearing shorts, T-shirts, and bibs with lobsters printed on them. As we approached the tent I realized that I was grossly overdressed, and I begged Cosmas to let me go home and change, or just go home. In New York it was better to be overdressed than underdressed, but I didn't think that was going to be the case here; here I was going to be the new guy's overdressed wife who had obviously never been to a clambake before.

He reminded me that New Englanders were not quite as judgmental as New Yorkers. I let him know that New Yorkers weren't necessarily more judgmental than everyone else—okay, maybe they were, but I liked to think of it as being discriminating—but *everyone* across the country reads *US Weekly* (though maybe they didn't actually lie in wait for the mailman on Saturdays for it like I do), so everyone understands the concept of the fashion police and the fact that I was going to get a big fat citation on this particular Saturday (failure to dress within bounds of particular social occasion—it's not as if I was Sharon Stone and could pull it off). He gave me his hello-who-are-we-talking-about-here-and-don't-you-know-that-doctors-have-more-important-things-to-do-with-their-time-than-read-silly-celebrity-magazines look. Oh please. Whenever you go to any doctor's office, how come the most recent issue of *US* or *People* is never ever in the waiting room? The doctor is running late due to scheduling? Ha! The doctor is running late because just like everyone else he's reading about Gwyneth Paltrow's current love interest. Everybody reads those magazines, even doctors. Cosmas told me I was being paranoid and said it would be fine.

I was then thrust into the crowd and was nodding my head, smiling politely, and shaking hands firmly—but not too firmly—and soon I realized that my high heels kept slowly sinking into the lawn. So depending on when you met me, I was anywhere between five foot four and five foot seven. I had a little chant going in my head to the rhythm of the McDonald's Big Mac song, "Nod, nod, smile and shake, unstick right, then left . . . icy Coke, thick shake, sundaes, and apple pies." Cosmas gave my hand a squeeze and whispered that I was humming, which I promptly stopped.

When we had first emerged from the car I had heard in my head a drum roll as the curtain rose on my debut as a wife. I was the type who usually blossomed in social occasions, and I was primed and ready. I would be the one who would sparkle with laughter at my husband's jokes, the one who would dazzle the crowd with my witty remarks and my keen observations—I had some of my most flattering Cosmas stories ready and waiting, in case I found an opening. I was going to take this clambake by storm; by the end we'd all be dancing on the tables, choreographing our own dance routine called the lobster, and swishing our tails and snapping our pincers. They'd all joke with me as we kissed good-bye on both cheeks that next year I'd have to remember to wear red and bring castanets. By God, this clambake was going into the shellfish hall of fame.

I was going to take this clambake by storm; by the end we'd all be dancing on the tables.

As I unstuck and shook, unstuck and shook, the drum roll petered out. There had been no buildup, no solo in the spotlight, and certainly no grand finale. Sure, to me this event was a big deal, but to everyone else I was just the new doctor's wife. No one seemed all that interested in my funny stories or in me. It was obvious that there would be no Academy Award for me as leading lady, or even as best supporting actor. When the credits rolled, I'd be listed simply as "overdressed wife #1."

In the car on the way home I was silently critiquing my forgettable performance, feeling a little as if I might have let Cosmas down. Cosmas was nervously tapping the steering wheel, and he kept glancing over at me. I knew he was trying to figure out whether he had done something wrong, and if he had, he didn't want to open the door to a hailstorm by saying something like, "Did I do something wrong?" I could tell that he was silently going through a checklist of things that would have possibly upset me at a party—he hadn't abandoned me, he had remembered to get me drinks, he had introduced me to the few people whom he knew, and he had often put his arm around me or grabbed for my hand. Once he knew he was in the clear he took a tentative first step and commented that the clambake had been nice and that he couldn't remember the last time he had eaten such fresh corn.

I nodded but didn't really say anything. He asked if I wanted to debrief, which was usually my favorite part of any social outing. It was always fun to pick apart the evening and talk about everyone we'd met. We'd discuss who was flirting with whom and what people were wearing, and then we'd run through highlights of some of the more interesting conversations that we had had. I sort of shrugged and just continued to look out the window. The suspense was killing him, so he blurted it out, "Are you mad at me?" I shook my head no, and his relief was visible as his hands relaxed a bit on the steering wheel.

Finally, I told him that I didn't have anything to debrief; no one had really talked to me all that much. Everyone's questions had been the same: when did we move to Boston, where do we live, and how were we finding Boston. Then they would make some crack about the fact that once his job started I was never going to see him again, which I knew was true, but I didn't really think it was polite to rub my face in it. I had even tried volunteering that we had just gotten married and that this was one of my first social occasions as a new wife, but that didn't evoke much of a response either. In fact, I told him that I didn't think anyone really noticed me at all.

He told me that I was mistaken, that he had talked to someone who had definitely noticed me. And he said he knew someone else who had said that he was a really lucky guy to have me as his wife. That perked me up a bit, but I wasn't sure whether he was just saying it to make me feel better. So I asked, "Who said you're lucky to have me for a wife?"

He told me that when he went back for seconds, he had noticed that the guy who was serving the lobsters (the one wearing the chef's hat that had the front half of a lobster sticking out the front and the tail sticking out the back, not quite as funny as having an arrow go through the head, but whatever) was sort of looking over at me and had asked him whether I was his wife. Cosmas had said that, yes, he was the lucky guy to have me for his wife. (Like that counts; this is comparable to your mom saying that you were the best one in the music recital.)

Later that night when we were watching TV it occurred to me that I hadn't asked him what exactly the lobster guy had said about me. Cosmas sort of shrugged and said that I really didn't want to know. He then faked a yawn, turned off the TV, and was just about to make a quick getaway when I told him to freeze and demanded to know what the lobster guy said when Cosmas said he was lucky to have me as his wife. He looked at me point-blank and asked if I was sure I wanted to know.

I racked my brain for any infractions on my part; what was he alluding to? What faux pas did the lobster guy have on me? I hadn't flirted with anyone else. I hadn't even eaten a lobster (soooo messy, and the sound effects, ick), so it's not as if I could have done it incorrectly with the wrong pinky-finger position. I had brought a gift, I had thanked our hosts at the end. Nothing. As far as I could tell I was in the clear. I asked again, in a toned-down if-you-expect-to-get-any-sleep-tonight-you-better-tell-me way. So he told me that the guy said he thought it was real classy that I had sneaked into the woods to smoke (arghhhhh, busted!) and joked that I looked as if I was dressed for the Academy Awards as opposed to a New England clambake. Cosmas just stood there in a conflicted pose, not sure whether to get on my case for the smoking, which he had every right to do (I knew I should have walked back to the car!) or whether he should be ready to comfort me in case I got upset that the fashion police turned out to be the lobster guy.

I sat there for a moment, also unsure of how to proceed, because I really didn't want to get into the whole "bad, bad Jenny smoking" discussion (because if ever I needed a cigarette it had been that afternoon), and, as for the lobster guy, well, I must say he was better dressed for the part than I that day, and he was right. I didn't know how to dress for a clambake, but I knew I'd do better next year. So I faked a yawn myself, got off the couch, put my hands around Cosmas's waist, and said that we should do the "lobster" across the kitchen to go brush our teeth (my charming way of suggesting we just forget the whole subject entirely). He began to wave his hands in the air like snapping pinschers, and I shook my tail.

WHAT'S MINE IS YOURS AND WHAT'S YOURS IS MINE, BUT PLEASE DON'T USE MY SHAMPOO

Cosmas is one of those people who *loves* his morning shower. I honestly didn't know what he could possibly find to do in there for so long. He's tried to explain it to me, but I just don't get it. My showers last only five minutes, unless I am deep-conditioning my hair, and even then I sometimes get out of the shower to multitask by shaping my eyebrows or applying a face mask. I know it's supposed to be sexy and romantic to take showers together, but we've tried and have found that we are completely incompatible from everything to the temperature, to the duration, to the direction in which we clean—I mean, it makes no sense to go from bottom to top, does it?

Another problem we run into while showering together is that we both happen to be backseat bathers, each telling the other how to wash—Cosmas shampoos his hair for too long and then doesn't condition for long enough. He tells me that my lathering abilities are abysmal and shows me that if you twirl the soap in your hand like fifty million times you get a nice thick foam (yeah, and you go through a bar of soap every three days). I informed him the best way to wash his face is in small circles as opposed to a vigorous up and down scrubbing motion. He explained to me that Gillette spent millions of dollars in R&D to design the perfect razor for the male face and that my using it to shave my legs was a slap in the face to engineers everywhere. Finally, after we bumped heads for the umpteenth time (I kept telling him that whoever dropped the soap should pick it up. No need for chivalry in a space that's a foot and a half by four feet), we swore off dual showers forever. The most we ever did was a two-ships-passing-in-the-night scenario (one person stepping in when the other was stepping out). Once he slapped my butt and yelled, "Iceberg!" which I thought was funny until he took the joke one step too far and made a crack about it being big enough to sink the *Titanic*. Talk about calling in a death wish. (My iceberg and I froze him out for two days after that one.)

We have now settled into a comfy routine of my hanging out in the bathroom while he showers and just talking through the curtain. It is a good time to catch up with one another since we are both so busy and his schedule is so erratic with his patient work and ongoing lab experiments.

I have also found that it is the perfect forum for introducing new ideas (Cosmas is a creature of habit), and he is always a bit more receptive to new ideas as he splashes happily in the shower. A few months ago we had even developed a weekly ritual during which I would tell him about new arty movies that had opened, reading out loud parts of the rave reviews. He then pretended he was interested and said that we would definitely go during the upcoming weekend. But when Friday rolled around he would flash his big doe eyes and beg off, asking if we could see whatever new Hollywood blockbuster had just come out instead.

It was during one of these steamy morning chitchat sessions that I discovered he was using my shampoo. It

It was during one of these steamy morning chitchat sessions that I discovered he was using my shampoo.

never occurred to me that this kind of transgression could be happening in my own home without my having an inkling that something was wrong. I am one of those women who can't walk into a drugstore without cruising the hair/body/face product aisle. So there are at least three other types of shampoo in the shower, as well as three different types of conditioner. My shampoo and conditioner, my facial cleanser, and my body wash are all huddled together in one corner—*my* corner. I never even would have noticed except that I dropped the lid to my facial toner and it rolled behind the toilet. As I reached down to get it I saw in my peripheral vision, through the space between the shower curtain and the wall,

I was now sitting up on my knees on the floor, transfixed by the scene before me.

that Cosmas was bending toward my corner and appeared to be reaching for *my* shampoo. I held my breath, thinking that maybe he would soon realize his mistake and exchange it for one of the other bottles that were ready and waiting in every other corner of the tub, but that didn't happen.

I shrank back in horror and watched the Hitchcock-like scene unfold in a shadowy silhouette before me: there he was opening the bottle of my shampoo—the shampoo that was very, very expensive; the shampoo that was very, very hard to find; the shampoo that was rich, creamy, and chock-full of exotic hair nutrients that can be found only in tropical rain forests (hence the hefty price, as rare jungle plants are very, very expensive)—the shampoo that specifically stated you are supposed to use only a small amount for maximum results (the size of a quarter to be exact). I watched as he turned the bottle upside down, gave it the hearty shake used for a cheap diner's ketchup bottle, and squeezed it right in the center. I recoiled. That was no quarter-size-dollop-producing squeeze, that squeeze was bigger than even a silver dollar. That squeeze was like a serving of Dairy Queen soft serve! I was now sitting up on my knees on the floor, transfixed by the scene before me. He proceeded to lather up his hair, and I could hear awful wet sucking noises and see a mountain of foam rising from his prodigal dollop of shampoo.

No wonder his showers took so long, it took him ten minutes just to get all the shampoo out of his hair. We were now at that part in the movie when I was on the floor, paralyzed with horror, and the entire audience was screaming at the screen, "RUN! RUN! JUST GET UP OFF THE FLOOR AND RUN, YOU IDIOT!" My left hand was over my chest ready to pound it if my heart didn't start beating again soon, and my right hand was clapped over my eyes. I peeked out through the cracks and watched him bend and reach for my conditioner. Again, a monster squeeze. He rubbed it into his hair for like two seconds and then immediately started to rinse! WHAT IS HE DOING? YOU'RE NOT SUPPOSED TO PUT IT IN YOUR HAIR AND IMMEDIATELY RINSE IT OUT. DOESN'T HE REALIZE THAT THE THIRTY TROPICAL BOTANICAL RAIN-FOREST

ENZYMES NEED SOME TIME TO WORK? THEY'VE GOT TO GET IN THERE AND START REPAIRING THE DAMAGE; THEY'VE GOT TO WEAVE THEIR SILKEN POLYMERS AROUND EACH INDIVIDUAL HAIR TO STRENGTHEN IT, ADDING EXTRA RESILIENCE FOR A NICE HEALTHY BOUNCE. HE MIGHT AS WELL JUST POUR THE WHOLE BOTTLE STRAIGHT DOWN THE DRAIN!

Just then the phone rang, and I assumed it was an early-bird telemarketer; normally I would have let the machine get it, but this time I sprinted for the phone. Quick, sell me luggage-protection insurance! Any diversion would do; I just couldn't witness his next blatant crime against beauty. I was surprised and overjoyed that it happened to be my best friend, Laura, on the line, which was perfect because she is a hair guru—I mean, she is a woman who knows hair. She knows color, she knows products, and she can tell you from fifty paces the make, model, and features of any blow dryer you show her. I'm not joking. It's the best party game. We used to show up at someone's apartment, and I would root around in their bathroom, invading their privacy, until I found their blow dryer, and then I'd walk out into the living room where she was getting a drink. I'd yell out, "Blow dryer, three o'clock" and she'd whip around, glance at it, and yell out its stats: "Conair, 1996, three air settings cold, warm, and a thermal heat blast button, comes in black, red, and silver, and has two attachments." Believe me, she is an East Coast legend.

As soon as I realized it was her, I asked how she knew to call me just then, convinced that she must have had a sixth sense when it came to hair emergencies. She was actually calling for my thoughts on the whole baby blue or metallic green toenail polish trend because she was getting a pedicure before work. I said that if she wanted to go wacky for a week, she should think about something nontraditional like lavender with a tinge of metallic sparkle, but the whole blue-green thing just didn't do it for me; besides we were no longer in our early twenties. Then I explained my emergency in progress. She demanded, "Well, did you stop him?" I told her that I had choked and had been completely unable to do anything. Aghast, she yelled at me, "You mean you just sat there and let it happen? You're one step away from accessory to the crime."

In my defense, I said that I thought maybe the rules were different now that we were married. I mean, didn't we have to share everything? Wasn't there some sort of what's-mine-is-yours-and-what's-yours-is-mine clause in the marital contract? Wouldn't he think that I was being selfish for not sharing? She asked me how much hair I had. I was confused, and she just repeated the question. I told her that it was pretty long these days, about midback. Then she asked me how much hair he had. I mumbled that he had maybe an inch and a half, two, tops. She told me that two inches of hair did not require the good stuff, even though he did have much nicer hair than most men, but still . . . She told me I had to put a stop to it right away. I asked her if something similar had ever happened to her, and she said yes, but she had stopped her fiancé, Chris, while in the act, grabbing his wrist and twisting until he fell to his knees and dropped the bottle. She warned him that if she ever caught him near her shampoo again he'd be going on their Hawaii honeymoon alone. She told him in no uncertain terms that he was never to use her shampoo, and if he felt that he needed a specialty shampoo for a specific hair issue he was experiencing, she'd be happy to go to the local drugstore and help him select an appropriate product. I asked whether he had minded, and she said of course not, because boys didn't care about their hair—well, unless they were losing it.

She warned me that if I didn't nip this situation in the bud right now, it could develop into a very serious problem; before I knew it he'd be demanding a cashmere bathrobe and his own loofah. I asked her whether it could be a fluke and explained that I had plenty of other shampoos in the shower and had never noticed him using mine before. She then grilled me on how many ounces were in my standard bottle, the size of my recommended dollop, and the number of times I washed my hair a week. I heard her tapping her Visor calculator, and she soon announced that I should be going through a bottle every two and half months. Hmmm, she had me there, because I remembered buying a new bottle a month and a half ago, and I was already getting dangerously close to the end again. Did I need any more proof than that? It was either him or some wild shampoo thief was on the loose.

She said that if I really felt I needed more proof, I could always mark the bottle with a sharpie and monitor the level for a week, but she thought this was unnecessary and pushed for an immediate confrontation. She reassured me that he'd probably be fine with it, and besides it was wasteful to have him use it when there are so many women out there who would give an internal organ for such a luxury. When I asked her if I should tell him how much it cost, she informed me that was a catch-22; he could get upset just based on the price alone, since men will never understand how much cash it takes to look good. I thanked her for her advice and promised I'd let her know what happened.

When I walked back in the bathroom to talk to him, I found him rubbing lotion into his hands. One quick sniff and I nearly fainted. He was using my Crème de La Mer moisturizer on his hands.

Was he mad? La Mer was probably the most expensive moisturizer on the planet at 120 bucks for a teeny tiny bottle. I myself only used the size of a small pea three times a week and on national holidays, and here he was using what appeared to be something along the size of a brussels sprout. As he was just about to put three fingers back in the jar again I lunged for it, snatching it out of his hands, and we both yelled out "What are you doing?" at exactly the same time.

I waved the jar around in the air and bellowed that this was facial moisturizer and was never to be used on hands. He told me his hands were dry, and I said fine, he should use the Lubriderm that was sitting on the back of the toilet, practically waving its nozzle at him, begging to be used. He said he didn't like the way it smelled. I told him that it was unscented lotion and, thinking he wouldn't want to smell like lotion, I bought it specifically for him. He said he liked the way the La Mer smelled. I told him that I was glad he liked it and that he

> **We both yelled out "What are you doing?" at exactly the same time.**

could smell it on me on Tuesdays, Thursdays, Saturdays, and any national holiday for which banks closed.

I explained that this was very special cream, basically one step away from a certifiable miracle. I told him how Heather Locklear used it all over her body, and before he could object, I told him that Heather Locklear was a millionaire and that as soon as we had ten million in the bank, he could take a bath in the stuff for all I cared. He wanted to know how much it cost, and I told him that no, he really didn't want to know, and since we were on the subject of extravagance, I would really prefer if he didn't use my shampoo and conditioner either.

The bathroom got so quiet I swear you could hear the condensation evaporating off the mirrors. I couldn't read his facial expression very well, but it looked like a composite of 30 percent hurt feelings, 30 percent righteous indignation, 30 percent disbelief because how much could one possibly pay for a teeny tiny jar of lotion, and 10 percent mild panic because he had this sneaking suspicion that he was late for work. He wasn't saying anything, so I felt as if I needed to make the first move, and I was seriously trying to come up with a tap dance number that would take me right out of the room. I swallowed hard and said, "Ten inches." He reacted with a squinty look that indicated there was no way he could possibly have any clue where I was going with this, so I should just continue. "It's just that I have at least ten inches more hair than you . . . and . . . and you're only supposed to use a quarter-size dollop of shampoo . . . less if you have less hair . . . and you, you used gobs, but what can you expect with a squeeze that could have choked a chicken, and the lather . . . tons of bubbles when I have maybe ten bubbles, which is one bubble per inch . . . and it's so hard to find, basically impossible . . . hours calling all over the city . . ." I wasn't making any sense and I knew it, but I was so racked with guilt over being silly enough even to have brought the whole thing up. I mean, Cosmas really did have fabulous hair, and not just for a guy. All the time my friends were commenting on it, and sometimes total strangers stopped him on the street; it was on a par with Hugh Grant's in the way it flopped ever so nicely across his forehead.

He finally realized that he had to say something, otherwise he'd never get to work that day. So he said, "Which shampoo are we talking about?"

My guilt vanished. If he didn't even know which shampoo was the good stuff, then he didn't have to use it anymore. I grabbed the shower curtain, yanked it aside, and pointed to my corner where my precious bottles were sitting. He looked over at them, nodded, and said that he was using them only because the smell reminded him of me. He told me how every now and then at work he'd get a little whiff of me when the air current moved just so and how it made me smile But, he said he certainly didn't have to use the shampoo anymore if I didn't want him to. He then kissed me on the forehead and trotted out of the bathroom.

That afternoon I threw out all the other bottles of shampoo and conditioner and stocked another two bottles of my shampoo and conditioner, or rather, *our* shampoo and conditioner, in the shower. I bought two kinds of scented lotion and hid my bottle of La Mer. I mean, who was I to stand in the way of love and good hair?

CHAPTER TWO

To Have and to Hold

A Living (Suburban) Legend

Everyone knows that urban legends are the grown-up versions of scary campfire tales—spooky stories that get passed around and are designed to teach you some lesson in life, like if you go parking with your boyfriend on a school night, then surely some maniac killer with a hook for a hand will come tapping on your window, or if you go home with some beautiful stranger in a bar, you might wake up in a bathtub full of ice missing a kidney. The first thing to clue us in that these tales are not real is the fact that all of these things happened to a friend of a friend's friend's fourth cousin. Second, no one can ever provide specific dates, names, and places. There was no guy making the rounds on the talk shows who lifted up his shirt and showed off his jagged scar where a kidney once lay, and as far as I know there's never been a young couple to come forward who can provide the bloody hook that once belonged to a crazed killer. So all in all I've never been too bothered by such stories.

Then there are the urban legends that target married people; I like to call them "suburban legends." Back in my single days I certainly heard a few of these suburban legends about the perfect wife, or the perfect husband, and, I gotta say, these little stories made the little hairs on the back of my neck stand up and my eyes widen, I would slap my hand down on the bar and say something like, "YOU ARE KIDDING ME! NO WAY! HOW THE HELL DOES ANYONE MAKE ONION DIP FROM SCRATCH? I THOUGHT EVERYONE USED THE LIPTON SOUP MIX. IT'S THE LAW. WHO IS THIS WOMAN? WHERE DOES SHE LIVE?" More often than not, I was very relieved to hear that this woman was from Connecticut and was the cousin of a friend of a friend of someone's sister's friend, which meant that the urban legend rules applied and no

Back in my single days I certainly heard a few suburban legends about the perfect wife.

such woman really existed. It was just a tall tale meant to scare the crap out of urban women who don't cook.

But, of course, scary stories tend to stay in the back of your mind, and I've even had some recurring nightmares about the Stepford wife. It always features the same thing: a perfect wife wearing a tidy, pressed, ruffled apron and smiling a huge smile with too many teeth. Everyone in the room is whispering about how amazing she is . . . she is president of the PTA, her desserts are always bought first at the bake sale, her house is spotless, her children are achingly polite, her dinners are gourmet, and she can bake a soufflé capable of reducing a grown man to tears. So in my dream I would be wading through an ocean of people in an enormous and extremely well decorated living room (a neutral theme—lots of ecrus and beiges with surprising accent pieces in cranberry and burnt orange), and as I am trying to make my way through the crowd, I hear everyone ooooh their approval of her choice in window treatments and then ahhhh over her recessed lighting and fancy dimmer switches.

Suddenly I'd feel as if I was suffocating, and I'd frantically try to make my way out of the room. At long last I would get to what I think is the door out, but it isn't; to make matters worse, it leads to the kitchen. Of course, the perfect wife would be in the kitchen, but she's no longer the petite size-four (same size since high school, thanks to Jane Fonda every morning) wife, she's a huge monster in a gigantic Laura Ashley dress (who knew they came in XXXL?) with hundreds of writhing arms each doing something different—stirring sauces, sautéing vegetables, frosting cakes, darning socks, folding sheets, basting chickens, cleaning the fingerprints off the walls by the light switches. . . . Talk about terrifying—usually this is when I would bolt awake, drenched in sweat and gasping for air. Hell, give me a guy in a hockey mask any day of the week.

The nightmare would vary a bit each time I had it; I always tried a different door to escape (I was no fool, not even in my dreams), but, of course, because it was a dream and annoyingly illogical, every door led to the kitchen. I was well aware that they were purely anxiety dreams and that the monster was a representational manifestation of my own insecurities—because the monster was only doing things that I felt at which I was not that great, as opposed to doing things about which I felt strong and confident. The monster wasn't ever playing poker, applying lip liner, or making microwave popcorn. Eventually, the nightmares subsided, and I managed to quell my fears by constantly reminding myself that these mythical "perfect wives" don't exist.

Then I met my neighbor, Mary Sue Sutton, the perfect wife (the ultimate southern belle transplanted to

New England—how interesting), who happens to be married to the perfect husband. My new secret code name for her—which I use when wanting to scare my hard-core urbanite friends with her honey-coated perfection—is Mrs. Mary Sunshine.

A few days after we moved into our current apartment she came knocking, bearing a basket of apples for me (we girls had to watch our figures) and a homemade apple pie for Cosmas. The pie smelled incredible, and I noticed it was still warm, so I asked whether there happened to be a bakery nearby. She smiled sweetly and said that she actually made the pie herself. I was amazed; I didn't think people really made pies anymore, well, at least not at home in an urban area. I took a closer look at the pie and marveled at its perfection—the intricately braided top layer looked machine made, the coloring was perfectly even, and there were razor-thin apple slices fanned in a 360-degree circle as the centerpiece. If it weren't a baked good, it could pass as art. This was obviously the work of someone who had a great deal of time on her hands, or someone who was as anal as they come, or perhaps both.

It was then that I realized she was still standing in the hallway. Embarrassed, I invited her in and offered her the only thing I had available, which was a chair. So while

I started looking around for the box that contained our glasses so that I could offer her some of Massachusetts's finest tap water, I thought about the fact that Cosmas would probably foam at the mouth when he came home and saw the pie—apple pie was, of course, his most favorite dessert in the entire world (obviously Mary was also equipped with some sort of radar). I had difficulty trying to come up with something to say to her. I guess I felt that anyone who could make a pie had to be my polar opposite, so we'd probably have nothing in common. I

If there's one thing those southern women can do, it's bake.

started with the fact that I, myself, had actually been born and lived in Tennessee (up until I was finally able to get the hell out of there). She drawled a surprised, "Reeeaaaaally, I wouldn't have ever known it. You seem so very Yankee-like." I had no clue whether that was a compliment or an insult, so I wasn't sure how to respond, I didn't really want to proceed in this direction for fear that she'd invite me over to see her Confederate flag collection. So I asked whether she had been baking long? She said she started at age six, putting her Betty Crocker toy oven to good use. I smiled at this because I, too, had had a toy oven as a little girl, but while I had been putting out the standard cupcake, Mary was more than likely producing four-tiered wedding cakes for her Barbie's dream wedding. If there's one thing those southern women can do, it's bake. I was probably the only girl in my high school who couldn't make a croissant from scratch.

Next she told me how when she was ten years old she planted an apple tree from a few seeds in her backyard, and, of course, the thing grew into an enormous tree; every year she and her husband, Peter, flew south to pick apples. She then turned into a human apple-baking machine: pies, tarts, breads, muffins, jams, cakes—you name it, and she's thrown an apple in it and baked it. Just as I was thinking she probably had a little ring binder filled with apple recipes, I heard her say, "Peter, my husband, gave me a darlin' little recipe book for Christmas. It has a big ol' Granny Smith apple on the cover, and I filled it with all my apple recipes."

I suppose there are times in your life when you come across someone who is basically yourself but turned inside out and backward.

I honestly didn't think I was a person who compared herself to others, and I have certainly never wanted to be anyone else but me (well, maybe Madonna in the era of "Express Yourself" and "Vogue," but didn't every girl?)

but I suppose there are times in your life when you come across someone who is basically yourself but turned inside out and backward. She was blonde, sweet (in a honeysuckle-bush-on-a-hot-summer-day way), and I detected absolutely no trace of sarcasm or extended therapy. She was also totally put together. Granted, her style was a little too southern country club for me, but she did know how to dress to show off her best features—her big chest (need you ask?) and her golden honey hair. Of course, at that moment, anyone would look fashionable next to my dirty T-shirt, jeans, and unwashed hair.

There was an aura about her, and I just knew she'd dominate the kitchen of any apartment or house that she ever visited, the same way Tiger Woods dominates every golf course he plays. I took a deep breath as my apartment was already starting to smell like warm apples, butter, and cinnamon—and the smell was emanating not only from the pie but from her—I mean, the woman grew her own apples for heaven's sake. I certainly had never grown a fruit before, though once I made a raisin, and that was only because I didn't believe my brother when he told me that raisins were just dried grapes. So I put a grape in a drawer, forgot about it for a few months, and eventually discovered my creation. I'm pretty sure I never even thought to make a scone with it; I probably just threw it away.

I was pulled back to the present by a flash of memory that made me break into a wide smile; I just remembered that Cosmas's favorite dessert wasn't apple pie. Cosmas's favorite dessert was actually apple pie with vanilla ice cream (he was a total à la mode man who liked ice cream with everything, wink-wink). A-ha! Take that, Mrs. Mary Sunshine. Maybe you know how to bake a pie, but I know how to serve it. I had an image of myself wearing some of my honeymoon lingerie while serving him pie in bed. WAIT A SECOND! WHAT WAS HAPPENING TO ME? WHY WAS I SUDDENLY FEELING SO CRAZILY COMPETITIVE WITH THIS PERFECTLY NICE WOMAN? SHE WAS JUST TRYING TO BE A GOOD NEIGHBOR. IT WASN'T AS IF SHE WAS AFTER MY HUSBAND.

I came out of this bizarre reverie to hear her say, "When I was leaving for my aerobics class this morning, I saw your husband. Quite dashing, and such great hair."

This caused me to drop the paper cup of water I had just managed to scrounge up, and, of course, I hadn't a clue where the paper towels were (the kitchen was getting unpacked last—seriously, what's the rush?). I twirled about feverishly, knocking things over, looking for anything with which to wipe up the spill when Mary—with the speed of a superhero—spotted the roll on top of the boxes on top of the refrigerator, jumped up, pulled off a few sheets, performed some move that was one step away from an Olympic gymnastics short program, and wiped up the water. I smiled. "Cheerleader?" She smiled back. "Something like that." Ahhh, those southern women, they were raised right, able to exude mystery and charm over the simplest things. I had learned a few tricks myself but had obviously left town before I mastered all the moves. Probably Mary has never had to open a door for herself in her entire life, and her role model is Scarlett O'Hara.

"Yes," I finally managed to reply to her obvious lust for my husband, "Cosmas is a great guy, and he does have great hair. It wasn't always so nice though; a few months ago it was sort of dull and lifeless, but I spent a lot of time researching specialty shampoos and tracked down this botanical rain-forest shampoo and conditioner that totally revitalized it. Yes, only the best for my honey." WHAT WAS I DOING? WHY DID I FEEL COM-PELLED TO LIE TO HER? Obviously her presence was waking up some deep-rooted insecurity that I had about my abilities in the domestic arts. I knew I had to get a grip, so I tried to change the subject. Suddenly the image of South Fork popped into my head, and I asked her if she rode horses. She said that yes, in fact she owned one, and she stabled it at Peter's parents' farm in Connecticut, which is where they used to live. I nodded because this made sense to me; of course she can bake a pie because what else is there to do when you live on a farm? So I asked whether she meant farm the way a lot of New Yorkers meant farm—a massive rustic country house that sat on a hundred acres of prime real estate, complete with clay courts, and a black-bottomed pool, or was she talking farm as in *Green Acres:* big red barn, chickens, and churning your own butter. She said yes to the acreage, barn, and the butter, but there were no chickens.

I blinked a few times and thought about what she had just said. Had I heard her correctly? Did she actually know how churn her own butter? I knew I should let it go—who cared if she churned butter—but I couldn't. "So you actually know how to make butter? Like a stick-of-butter-wrapped-in-foil stick of butter?" She said that she didn't really make sticks, more like a big block that you could cut into squares, but she had tried to carve a block into the shape of a duck once, but it had ended up looking more like a hedgehog with wings. (Hedgehog?) So that's when I asked her if she had been to that restaurant in New York that served butter in the shape of ducks, and she squealed because that's where she had gotten the idea. How funny. Small world. She confessed that since there wasn't much to do on the farm, she'd decided to make the best of things and to learn everything: she could milk a cow, chop firewood, drive a tractor, and make sour cream and cheese.

We then got into a lengthy discussion of *Little House on the Prairie* and the fact that Caroline Ingalls happened to be one of her role models. I totally agreed with her as I had always felt that Caroline left even June Cleaver in the dust when it came to being one of TV's greatest wives. Think about it. She was a great mother who never raised her voice, she was a magnificent cook, her house was spotless, and she still managed to keep her bun looking tidy—all this on a very tiny budget. By this time we were both screaming with laughter, and I had to admit that Mary Sunshine and I were maybe more alike than I originally thought, well, except for the fact that she could render lard.

It was what she said next that really made me feel that our meeting was fated. She told me that she went to the farm every other month to make a batch of sour cream and that she'd be happy to show me how it was done. She told me it was easy and that homemade sour cream was so much better than store-bought, and that these days she couldn't bear to make her special party onion dip without it.

Right then all those little hairs on the back of my neck stood straight up, and I clapped my hand over my mouth to hold back my scream. "What did you say?" I asked in a choked voice.

She repeated how fresh sour cream was actually better than store-bought; it was all in the texture. I shook my head and said that no, I wanted to hear about the onion dip.

So she told me that she was sort of famous for this special sour cream onion party dip over which people apparently swoon and for which everyone always begs for the recipe, but that her great-aunt, who told it to her, made her swear that she would pass it along to only two people in her lifetime—"one relative and one non" so it could maintain its allure and mystery.

It was her. She was the one. Not only had I just met a living suburban legend, but she lived right next door to me.

"So you don't use Lipton onion soup mix?" I asked. Now it was her turn to look horrified, and she let out a little "Gosh no," which was exactly the way I imagined mice and fairy-tale maidens to talk in bedtime stories. No sirree, her onion dip required four different types of onions (there are four different kinds?) that were minced, sautéed in seasoning, and folded into sour cream. She said that where everyone went astray was in mixing onion dip and serving it right then and there, but her recipe called for it to sit for at least forty-eight hours so the flavors could mingle.

That's it. That's all I needed to hear. It was her. She was the one. She certainly looked the part—the hair, the perkiness, and the having lived in Connecticut. Not only had I just met a living suburban legend, but she lived right next door to me. With a shaky and incredulous voice, I told her that five years ago at a party in New York I had heard about her onion dip, so it truly was famous. She actually blushed and said that she had received serious offers for the recipe, but that she refused even to consider selling it. She said this was partly out of superstition because when it came right down to it, she knew that she was pretty talented in a kitchen (clearly she had no idea that her presence made a kitchen hum with happiness) and she really did love to cook, but she was afraid that if she ever did something "evil" with her talents (like make money, or sabotage another woman's figure), she'd lose her abilities. She tittered at herself after telling me this, and she said she didn't even know why she had just told me that since she had never before told anyone her silly little fear, not even Peter.

I grinned and told her that I had that effect on people, and that having spent a lot of time in the bars of

New York, I have had quite a bit confessed to me in my day. I was virtually a talk-show host waiting to happen. I also told her that I, too, believe in fate and superstitions to a degree, and hers sounded reasonable (especially since stealing away another person's husband with pie would definitely rank in the "evil" category). Obviously she was a goddess in the kitchen, and by all means it must be a sin to use baked goods for the dark side.

Before I could really absorb all we had just talked about, before I could figure out whether my life had just changed for the better or worse (clearly my waistline was in trouble), Cosmas walked in the door, calling out, "Honey, I'm home; it smells delicious in here. Did you bake me a pie?" Then he burst out laughing, knowing that my baking was an impossibility but that teasing me about my cooking skills, or lack thereof, was pretty funny. I had been working with him for a while on his sense of humor, but I was hoping that this new thing of cracking himself up was just a phase. He stopped short when he zeroed in on the pie, and only after he licked his lips did I see him notice Mary.

I introduced them, but Cosmas didn't give Mary Sunshine a second glance; he was totally entranced by the pie. Mary then said her good-byes, telling me she had such a wonderful time meeting me and promising to drop off a batch of her onion dip the next time she made it. I walked her to the door and thanked her for her pie and the apples.

Later, over pie and ice cream (best thing we ever tasted), I told Cosmas all about my visit with Mary. I told him about her making her own butter, about the apple tree and the farm, and finally about her onion party dip that proved she was a suburban legend. Thankfully, Cosmas did not seem as impressed with her as I was, though he was pleased that we lived next door to someone who could make pie. Finally, I admitted to him that Mary made me feel incredibly insecure about my own status as a domestic goddess, and that I wasn't sure whether I hated her or wanted to be her. His answer was simple: He didn't give a flip about where I ranked on the culinary-arts food chain, since he obviously hadn't marry me for my cooking (hardy har har). As for my

Mary made me feel incredibly insecure about my own status as a domestic goddess.

hating her or wanting to be her, Cosmas said neither seemed right—from the way I talked about her, I clearly didn't hate her, and as for wanting to be her, he said no way. He wouldn't ever want me to be her. In fact, there was only one thing he'd trade me in for—uh-oh, here comes joke number three. But I knew what he was going to say, and before he could finish his thought, I handed him a second piece of pie. So we now know that the old saying about the way to a man's heart being through his stomach is partially true; luckily, however, there seems to be a clause in it saying that it doesn't matter if you're the cook or just the server.

As I watched him polish off his second piece of pie à la mode, I thought about what he said and knew he was right. I didn't hate Mary Sunshine and, of course, would never want to be her (I look horrible in gold), so that left only one thing—to befriend her. I'd have all my old city friends quaking in their stilettos with the stories I'd be able to tell, and, who knows, maybe I'd get to finish my southern education after all. All we'd have to do was find a West Coast Hollywood vixen, and we'd have a chance at rivaling Charlie's Angels as a special elite crime-fighting team.

THE TAMING OF THE SHREW (TO NAG OR NOT TO NAG . . . THAT IS THE QUESTION)

I have always woken up early and that particular morning wasn't any different, even though we had stayed up late unpacking his boxes. We were finally together and in our very first apartment. This was no slumber party, this was forever. So on this very first morning, I couldn't help but sit there and stare at him for the first ten minutes or so. I remembered how I used to try to wake him up early just because we always had so little time together and I felt that every waking moment counted, but I didn't have to wake him up on that morning because he wasn't going anywhere. We lived together now. We were married.

Eventually I got up and walked into the kitchen to get a glass of orange juice, and I was sort of humming and looking out the window, feeling very Disney movie–like, when I noticed that someone had left the bread bag open on the counter. Sitting next to the bread was a jar of mustard with the top off, and next to the bread was a mustard-covered knife lying on clean kitchen towel. I did that thing where you sort of rubbed your eyes in disbelief and moved in closer to inspect the damage. Now, I'm no Mrs. Clean, mind you, and I've been known to leave dirty dishes in the sink overnight, okay for a few nights even, BUT I WOULD NEVER, EVER PUT A MUSTARD-COVERED KNIFE ON A CLEAN KITCHEN TOWEL. It's just not done; in fact, I don't think I could even say that I have ever known anyone who would do such a thing—until now.

I wasn't sure what the proper protocol was in this particular situation. Now, if we were single and this was his apartment and his towel, I would probably just roll my eyes and say something like, "He's such a boy." Then I'd probably close the bread, throw away the mustard, and throw away the towel. Now, if we were single and this was my apartment and my towel, I'd say something like, "Ooooh, he's gonna get it." I'd close the bread, grab the mustard towel and knife, march into the bedroom, climb up on the bed, stand over him, and drop mustard blobs on him until he would wake up howling and then pull me down and tickle me until I begged mercy. But now I was married, now I had expensive French sheets, now I had to handle this situation in exactly the right way or I'd be cleaning up after him and washing mustard off kitchen towels for the rest of my life.

But now I was married, now I had expensive French sheets, now I had to handle this situation in exactly the right way.

So I decided not to clean everything up; instead, I left everything exactly as it was. I would just wait until he got up and then I'd let him clean up his own mess. It had been late last night and he had probably been overly tired from moving and had just slipped up. So I went and got the paper and read it in bed next to him until he woke up. I hung out with him while he brushed his teeth and talked to him through the shower curtain. When he went into the kitchen, I didn't follow him in. I got dressed because we were going to explore our new neighborhood together. When he came back into the bedroom, I smiled brightly, walked out mumbling something about needing a hair clip from the bathroom, and proceeded to dash to the kitchen. Bread still open, mustard cap now resting on top of the jar but was not screwed on, mustard-covered knife still on towel, and now orange juice out and sitting on the counter, too.

I called him into the kitchen, didn't say anything, and swept my hand in front of the counter the way a game-show hostess gestures to the prize merchandise. Then I cheerfully waggled my finger in his face and walked out of the kitchen, leaving him to clean up. He followed me out. "What was that all about? I was planning on cleaning it up." I cringed. I couldn't believe it. There was this metallic tone in his voice—the tone that a husband uses when his wife is nagging him. A little defensive, a little nasal, and a little overly enunciated. How could it have started so fast? I hadn't even said anything, for God's sake. I made a promise to myself that when I got married I would not become a nag, and I refused to let it happen. Without missing a beat I casually said, "I knew you were going to clean it up; it's really no big deal. I just thought you might forget about it and we were about to go out and I thought you'd be bummed if you had left the orange juice out.

That's all." I went to finish getting dressed, once again leaving him to clean up the kitchen, which he did.

He never left another dirty knife on a clean towel but, after the number reached double digits, I stopped counting how many jars of condiments I threw out. He protested every time, trying to convince me that things didn't necessarily spoil overnight. I reminded him that I was from the South—where you learned from a young age that mayonnaise could turn a picnic potato salad into a deadly weapon—and I wasn't taking any chances. I tried to break him of the habit by attaching to the jars little smiley-face notes that said things like, "Hope you enjoy your sandwich, but please don't forget to put me back in the fridge! Thanks. Monsieur Dijon." He either didn't notice the note or read it and just didn't respond to the nice-guy approach. The next set of notes I made more threatening, saying things like, "Put me back in the fridge or else! Signed, Victor Mayo," or "You better put me back in the $%^$^!!@ fridge, jacko! Signed, Kickyourbutt Ketchup." These he found sort of amusing and they worked for a time, but after a while he relapsed, so I stopped buying condiments altogether. On the now-empty refrigerator door shelf, I taped a note that said, "If you can't use condiments responsibly, then you can't use them at all."

This time he came to me and said, "I got your note, very funny, ha-ha. But the next time you're at the store, can you get that honey Dijon mustard again, the one that was more Dijony than honeyish?"

Suddenly, I felt the anger mounting and was deciding whether I should start with his assumption that *I* was going to be the one going grocery shopping for his stupid mustard (did *he* not have two functioning legs?). Or whether I should start with his total disregard for the 50 trillion times I had let him know that his carefree condiment ways were driving me crazy. So now the question was whether I was supposed to just let loose and freak out on him, or whether I should take the high road once again and try not to adopt the tone of voice that would make me a nag. I

So now the question was whether I was supposed to just let loose and freak out on him, or whether I should take the high road.

swallowed hard because I could feel this tinny taste in my mouth. I opened my mouth, having decided to suck it up and try to be calm and rational about it, but when I did it was too late. I just sort of erupted against my will. IS IT SO HARD TO JUST PUT THE TOPS BACK ON THE JARS, ALL THE WAY ON, NOT JUST PLACED ON, NOT JUST PLACED ON WITH HALF A TURN, BUT

ALL THE WAY ON, SCREWED TIGHT SO THAT BACTERIA AND OTHER FLOATING MICRO-SCOPIC THINGS WON'T GET IN IT AND BREED? THEN AFTERWARD, EVEN THOUGH I'M SURE YOU'LL BE SO TIRED FROM THE BIG STRENU-OUS WORKOUT OF PUTTING THE CAP ON, PERHAPS YOU CAN FIND ANOTHER OUNCE OF STRENGTH TO PUT THE JAR BACK INTO THE FRIDGE. THIS IS NO JOKE THIS TIME. I WILL NOT CONTINUE TO CLEAN UP AFTER YOU LIKE THIS, DO YOU HEAR ME? I AM NOT YOUR MOTHER!" Right after I said it I clapped my hand over my mouth. My words had surprised even me, and the look on Cosmas's face was one I had never seen before—a cross between wonderment and fear. I must admit that I did find the whole experience surprisingly titillating; it had felt really good to get it off my chest. So was that it? Was I now officially a nag?

The only thing he managed to say in response was that he was pretty sure my yelling actually made his hair move. I took this response and his dazed look as a sign that on some level I had actually gotten through to him this time (even if it was only on the decibel level). I reasoned that perhaps the reason everyone nags is because it's the only method that has proven to work. I crossed the fingers of my left hand, knocked on our wood table, and hoped for the best.

I WAS RAISED TO BE EXTREMELY NEAT, always required to make my bed and to have my bedroom immaculate, by a mother who swore that a messy house actually gave her a headache. Naturally, when I went off to college, I revolted and became a complete slob; my dorm room and later my own apartment always had clothes strewn over the bed and had books and magazines stacked and cluttered on the floor and all the table surfaces. But as disorganized and unruly as I could be, Cosmas was worse.

Please let the record show that when I first met Cosmas, he was incredibly neat, so neat that when my mother happened to see his apartment, she whispered to me that I might as well break up with him now because there was no chance he would marry a messy woman like me. But everything changed when after med school he moved to New Haven for his residency and had to work crazy hours. When he actually had free time, he would use it for sleep or to see me, but never to clean. By the end of two years he had the stereotypical bachelor boy's apartment, equipped with stacks of old pizza boxes, unidentifiable sticky spots on the kitchen floor (one of them took my slipper off once), a bathtub in which you almost felt dirtier after you showered, and dust bunnies that were the size of actual rabbits.

My theory was that by living in such dismal circumstances for so long, he just got conditioned to it and acquired the ability not even to see the mess around him. I was able to laugh about it at the time—his messes had little impact on me because I was living in another state. But after it moved into my own thousand-square-foot apartment, it was no longer so amusing and cute. I became determined to test my theory—could he see the mess or not?—and then figure out a way to bring him back from the dark side.

Although I have had my own piggy moments, my messes always make sense.

Although I have had my own piggy moments, my messes always make sense. All my clothes are normally flung over the bed or the chair in our room when I am too busy (and lazy) to hang them up. I found Cosmas's clothes everywhere—ranging from the standard fare of boxers on the bathroom floor (or somewhere on the path toward the bathroom), to a pair of his pants and dirty socks on the floor at the base of the couch. (Sure, I believed that unbuckling the belt and pants after a big meal was acceptable in the privacy of one's home, but it scared me to see that such processes advanced with time and developed into "Hmmm, I'm feeling a bit full and restricted right this second, so I think I'll just take off my pants right here while sitting on the couch watching TV.") Don't even get me started on wet towels; it was obvious that wherever he happened to be when he felt that he was adequately dry or perhaps that the towel was now wetter than he was, he would just hang the towel on whatever surface area was closer—a chair, the coffeemaker, a doorknob, or just the floor. I made a notation that my husband (or, in this case, "the subject") was obviously unable to see the towel racks either.

Beyond clothes, there was the issue of food. I have always been scrupulously clean when it comes to food (same idea as mayonnaise, but think ants)—I was programmed from a very young age that dishes must be done immediately following any meal and my training even went so far as to include knowing that the dishes weren't done until the sink was wiped clean and the water that collected behind the faucet was wiped up as well (otherwise the mortar would suffer). Also, I wasn't used to seeing dirty plates anyway, because the life span of dirty plates in my mother's home was fifteen seconds or less. My mom is fast and thorough—she is a member of the old school where you actually wash the dishes before putting them in the dishwasher. Cosmas's habits with food were really quite astounding and were clearly related to his wet-towel syndrome. I had discovered glasses, plates, paper towels with crumbs on them everywhere imaginable—whenever I found something somewhere odd, I'd try to re-create what had been running through his mind (if there had been *anything* running through his mind). Here I am standing by the mantel and I have just finished my soda. Hmmm, now what should I do with my empty glass? Oh, I know, I think I'll put it on the mantel right next to our expensive vases, our crystal candlesticks, and our wedding photos. Yikes, I'm late for work, but I'm still drinking my orange juice. I know, I'll just bring it with me into the hallway, lock the door, and leave my empty glass on the steps outside. I mean, seriously, what was he thinking? That our apartment was a nightclub or movie theater where you could just eat and drink and discard the waste on the floor?

Forget the fork with unidentifiable dried crud that I found in the cup that housed MY VERY EXPENSIVE BLUE SQUIRREL MAKEUP BRUSHES; let's move on to the one habit that bothered me the most. My darling husband happens to be a big fan of pistachio nuts and olives, and, being a nice wife, I tend to keep readily available a constant supply of the foods that he enjoys. Now the problem with both of these foods is that they generate waste—the shells and the pits. So when you serve them, you normally have to offer people a place to discard said by-products, something like a napkin, or, if you were my mom, a crystal bowl in the shape of a nut that went alongside the nice wooden nut bowl. But even when Cosmas had such a container at his disposal, very few shells and pits wound up there.

These are just a few of the most interesting places where I have found empty shells and pits: the floor, underneath couch cushions, on the windowsill, in his pants and shirt pockets, in my shoes, in the cup where I keep quarters for laundry, in my desk drawer, under the bed, in the bed, in the sink, and once I found a bunch of shells sitting on top of the TV, which probably meant he couldn't find the remote and must have stood there flipping channels and eating nuts. Now, if we were trying to give him the benefit of the doubt, believing that perhaps he might not have been able to see such small objects after innocently setting them down, after I found a half-eaten apple sitting on the couch, we can no longer extend him even that courtesy. He claimed to have fallen asleep while eating it, thereby causing it to roll off of him. In the beginning I would just pick up things as I found them and casually mention in a very friendly tone over dinner that I would appreciate it if he would start trying to clean up after himself a little more. I would then watch him scan the apartment to see if he could find what I was talking about. In a calm and nonnagging tone I would tell him that I had picked everything up, and I offered a few examples. He nodded and informed me that if I just left his mess for a while, he would eventually clean it up. (Funny, but that was what I used to say to my mom, so I guess what goes around comes around.) I bit my lower lip because I felt something rising in my chest, but I pushed it back down knowing that I had already tried that approach.

When I found an empty ice-cream bowl on top of the TV, I decided to conduct an experiment with it. I decided that I'd let it sit there and would wait until he found it and took it to the kitchen (giving him extra bonus points if he actually loaded it into the dishwasher). The first night—nothing. Night number two he watched TV for two hours—nothing. He watched TV the third night for three hours—still nothing. On the fourth day I tied a red ribbon onto the end of the spoon, wondering if that would get his attention and draw his eyes upward, but to no avail. Finally, on day five, after a patch of green fur began growing on the bowl, I issued him his first warning and let him know that he better shape up because

I was giving him only two more chances. He asked what would happen when he received three, and I replied that I had no doubt he'd find out soon enough.

His second warning came after three days' worth of Popsicle sticks accumulated on the windowsill next to the big reading chair. I tried to maintain my sense of humor and let him know that he was getting off easy because in some states he would have received a citation for each stick, which would have put him over his limit.

He did manage to make it almost two weeks before his third and final warning, which came when I realized that the orange juice glass that had been sitting in the bathroom for the past four days was now stuck to the back of the toilet. Every morning while he was brushing his teeth I'd be silently willing him to see the glass and return it to the kitchen. Before the fifth

Plan A was to admit defeat, surrender, and just start picking up after him. Plan B was to start nagging the heck out of him.

morning I placed his shaving cream alongside the glass, thinking that might do the trick. Nope. Well, it was settled, my theory about his being able to ignore completely what he didn't want to see was thereby confirmed.

Now I had to figure out what I should do next; the three verbal warnings had been just a way for me to stall for time until I figured out some brilliant plan of action. I figured that I didn't really have many options: Plan A was to admit defeat, surrender, and just start picking up after him. Plan B was to start nagging the heck out of him. And Plan C was to try to beat him at his own game, meaning I'd go on strike, which would entail my not only ceasing to pick up after him, but stopping picking up after myself as well.

What I learned was, Thou shalt not mess with the laws of housekeeping. I thought I was going to be teaching Cosmas a lesson, but what I did instead was jeopardize my own standards. My downfall was fast and furious. Imagine my sitting on the couch with a cup of coffee and a candy bar (breakfast). First, I unwrapped my candy bar and dropped the wrapper on the floor. Then I would happily eat my candy bar with my coffee. Afterward I'd get up off the couch, place the empty mug next to the dirty spoon on the coffee table, and go about my business. I had just saved at least five minutes since I didn't have to throw away the wrapper, rinse out my mug and spoon, and put them in the dishwasher.

When I took my shower, I just stripped down and left my clothes in a pile on the bathroom floor. After I finished, I stepped over my clothes, dried off, dropped my towel on the floor, and then went about my day. There was a huge feeling of freedom by not caring about such things, and it felt pretty good. Of course, I was taking it to an extreme level, so I didn't even do my dishes from lunch or throw away the empty Chinese take-out carton. Just as I suspected, after a surprisingly short time I no longer really saw the mess around me. It's surprisingly easy to push things aside to make room for the new.

I'm not sure if Cosmas would have noticed as fast as he did if I hadn't left the butter sitting on the counter. Yes, I get busy and rushed, too, and I have been known to leave everything everywhere under extenuating cir cumstances, but *never* would I *ever* have left a dairy product at room temperature unless something were really wrong. It is completely against my nature.

Cosmas may not be the quickest draw when it comes to noticing clutter around the house, but I gave him credit for knowing me well. He took one look at the butter and said, "Okay, what gives?" I feigned innocence, which involved scrunching up my brow and shrugging simultaneously, followed with making my mouth sort of round, as if to say, "Oh, whatever are you talking about?"

He started poking around the kitchen in an effort to understand. He examined the full sink of dirty dishes, the bread bag lying open, and the peanut butter and jelly jars both open and sitting on the counter. He moved on to the living room and peered at the newspaper on the floor, the candy wrapper by the couch, the coffee mug sitting on the windowsill. He went back into the kitchen, stared at the peanut butter and jelly jars for a while, and then gingerly screwed on the lids and put them back in the fridge. Next he closed the bread bag and put it away. Slowly he turned to face me, hanging his head a bit, and he apologized for leaving out the pb&j, for throwing the newspaper on the floor, and for leaving the coffee mug on the coffee table.

In utter disbelief, I wailed that it hadn't even been him who left out all that stuff, and duh!, he didn't even drink coffee! I told him it had been me—it was my mess and he better get used to it because as of that day I was officially on strike. If he didn't mind living in squalor and chaos then neither did I, because honestly what was the point of constantly cleaning up when the place just got messy over and over again, right?

Without a word he cleaned up the apartment.

He then had to work late a few nights in a row, and by the time he got a chance to take a good look around, I had managed to trash the place. What I had done in three days was far worse than anything Cosmas had ever done. All those years of being conditioned to pick up after myself and put away dairy products just evaporated in a few days of living like a scumbag. Why put my dirty socks in the hamper when I can roll them into a ball and try to see if I can hit the picture on the opposite wall with them?

He surrendered on Saturday after he spent two hours picking up the place. Raising his hands in the air, he waved around a white T-shirt. He swore that he had learned his lesson. I told him he had said that the last time. He said that all of this had been a wake-up call for him and he would really try harder, blah blah blah. I accused him of just saying stuff that he thought I would want to hear but not really being sincere. He asked whether I was just stalling for time because I liked being a slob and then offered me a pinky promise, which, of course, was more sacred than even a signed contract. Hmmm, he was right because I did secretly wish that I could be the slob for a few more days, as it really gave me so much extra free time, but as we all know, you can't turn down a pinky promise.

PILLOW TALK

I suppose it was inevitable once we were living together. Couples get into tiffs all the time, but for the first few months of our new living arrangements, we had good timing and were never in the position of being upset at each other late at night (probably too tired to care). So now we were about to do that thing you're not supposed to do, go to bed angry at each other. For some reason I had it in my head that in doing so we'd be marked for bad luck similar to what happens when you accidentally break a mirror. I briefly wondered whether the bad luck would get split evenly between us both, or whether it was determined based on a point system that took into account factors like who started it, who was most at fault, and whose idea it was to go to sleep without finding a resolution to the matter at hand. I yawned and thought that the superstition might arise from the fact that there was a grain of truth to the bad luck since the result of going to bed angry was probably waking up angry, and mornings are rough enough without having two grown people stomping around in a huff trying to get ready.

Unfortunately, most of the squabble took place in our bedroom, and since I was the one who was better at storming out of rooms—fists clenched, teeth gritted, long hair flowing—I was the one who ended up standing out in the living room. Drats. Me and my melodramatic streak. The storming-out thing worked much better when we didn't live together because I had more distance to storm—out the door, into a cab, off to my own apartment; by then my flash-flood temper would have run its course and I would call him, we'd make up, and then he'd come over to my place. This particular storm-out had carried me only twenty paces, and I was still irritated. I was left with two options—sleeping on the couch or going back into the bedroom I just stormed out of, which would probably lead to my having to say something first. I hated having to give in first; even when I had been the first one to call, I wouldn't say anything. I'd just get back to my apartment, call him, he'd answer the phone knowing it was me, and I'd just sit there in silence. Such a baby. I checked my watch and it was well past midnight. Both of us really needed to get to sleep. I really did not want to sleep on the couch, but I really didn't want to give in, either.

Maybe I could wait until he fell asleep, then crawl into bed afterward. I yawned; maybe I couldn't wait that long. So I stood up, thinking, Why should I get stuck on the couch; it was my bed, too. So I quietly walked back into the bedroom. He was sitting on the bed, on my side, reading a science magazine. Why was he on my side? Was this some type of defense strategy? Now I didn't know what to do because I was planning on just averting my eyes, getting into bed, and trying to go to sleep without saying a word. Now I *had* to say something because he was on my side. I wondered if he was smart enough to do this on purpose, knowing I'd have to say something. Hmmm, probably not; Cosmas is not as calculating as I am. I realized I was just standing in the middle of the room like a scared rat. I had to make a move. *Do something.*

In a panic I got into bed on his side and turned away so my back was facing him. I fidgeted around a bit and tried to puff up the pillows. They were flat; he always let me have the puffy pillows. I started to feel bad; perhaps I needed to buy a few more puffy pillows so he didn't get stuck with the flat ones. I tried to remember where I bought the puffy pillows to begin with. He let out a big sigh. Hmmm, what did that sigh mean? Was it a sad sigh or was it an angry sigh? I hope it wasn't a I've-really-had-enough-of-her sigh, surely not. So then he asked, "Would you prefer it if I slept on the couch?" His voice was quiet and sad.

Great, now he was within striking distance of being the martyr. He always gets to be the martyr; I should just have stayed out on the couch myself. He'd never let me stay on the couch, though. I tried it once when we were on vacation together, grabbing my pillow and the bed-spread and flouncing the six feet to the couch. He had come over and stood above me telling me that he wasn't going to let me sleep on the couch. So like a real mature person, I ground myself into the cushions and held fast to the armrest, refusing to budge as he tried to roll me off the couch. After a few minutes of this, he just lay down on the floor next to the couch. I told him to go back to bed, but he refused, saying that if I was going to sleep on the couch, then he would sleep on the floor. Not to be outdone, I then got up and lay on the floor next to him. We both lay there for a while staring at the ceiling; eventually we started laughing at the silliness of the situation and ended up making out. That was a pretty good fight.

So of course I didn't prefer him to sleep on the couch. Like I said, it wasn't really fair that he should have to sleep on the couch either. But what if he wanted to sleep on the couch as opposed to sleeping with me? Surely not, right?

So I said, "Only if you want to. I don't care." Ughhh, dammit, why did I have to go and say I didn't care? I didn't really mean it and now I had been a bit hostile. I bet I hurt his feelings. He was a pretty sensitive guy, and my temper caused me to be overly harsh at times. Hey, wait a second, why was I putting the blame on myself? He was as much to blame for the whole thing as I was. Still, I thought I needed to take back the I-don't-care part; it had been really unnecessary. Besides it wasn't even true.

"I'd like to take back the statement of 'I don't care' in my last response." Geez, what the heck was that? Who talked like that? It was as if I were asking to buy a vowel or something.

"So you do care?" his voice sounded a little bit better—hopeful and sweet, really. But why was he baiting me with these short provocative questions? Duh, of course I cared, but why should I have to admit it first? Why didn't he tell me that he cared and then ask if I cared? Yes, that would definitely have been better. I decided to ignore his question and ask my own question. Let me be the questioner for a change.

"Do you?" Ha. Take that! And my response question was even shorter than his—only two words. How did it feel to be on the receiving end, not so good, huh?

He replied, "More than you know." Ooooh, that was good. Very well done. Now it sounded as if we were in an old black-and-white movie. Why were those movies so much more romantic than the movies of today? Maybe it was a flashy lead-in to his apology; I waited. Maybe not. The ball was now back in my court. Now, how does one reply to "more than you know"? I mean, in some ways he was implying that I didn't realize how much he loved me, which was completely untrue. I was well aware of the magnitude of his love for me. Perhaps I should view that statement as hostile, because it could definitely be interpreted as sarcastic. Like he was better than me in some way. Maybe I should say that I loved him even more than that. I mean, I do. Well, I guess I couldn't say that I loved him any more than he loved me, because that wouldn't be very nice either. I think it was my turn to sigh. Sighs are very effective if done correctly. Should I sigh and say something? Or should I just sigh and leave it to inter-pretation on his end? Maybe I should take a more direct approach and just tell him that I didn't want him to sleep on the couch.

"No, I don't want you to sleep on the couch." Rats. I had forgotten to sigh first, and I couldn't sigh now because it wouldn't make any sense at all. It was so late; I needed to go to sleep. My brain hurt, and these pillows were unbelievably flat. Hell, I couldn't believe he had never said something about them. I bet prisoners had better pillows than these. Meanwhile, I had been luxuri-ating in puffiness; I even had two good pillows. Maybe my having to sleep on the flat pillows tonight was an appro-priate punishment.

Good, he was taking off his glasses and getting ready for bed. I closed my eyes and pretended to be asleep so I couldn't see him when he went to turn out the light. It was nice to have him turn out the light for a change, as it was usually my job since my side was closer to the light switch. I wondered if he looked at me. I wondered if he knew that I wasn't really asleep. He probably knew, because I almost never fell asleep before him. I wondered if I could even sleep on this side of the bed when I never had before. Well, that wasn't true. Once I slept on his side when he was out of town and I missed him; then I had wanted to sleep on his side, as if that would help. And it did help; actually, it made me feel better.

So now he was back in bed and his back was against mine, but not touching. He shifted around and I felt him tugging at my hard flat pillows, "Let's switch pillows, honey; I know you like the puffy ones." Wow, he really was so nice to me. Sometimes when it's hot out and I have used up all the cool sides of my pillows, he offers to switch pillowcases with me since he wasn't so particular regarding temperature issues. Now, that is love.

"No, that's okay, darling, you keep the good ones. I don't mind, really." Should I tell him that I was going to go the store tomorrow and get him new pillows? Perhaps I should keep it as a surprise.

"Honey, I insist, c'mon now, let's trade."

"Cosmas, it's fine. I don't mind using these tonight."

"You're being silly, let's just trade."

"No." I gripped the hard flat pillows closer. Great, now we were about to get into it again over pillows. This was so stupid.

"One for one?" he said softly. I smiled. That seemed fair, and honestly I really didn't know if I would even be able to sleep with these pillows.

"Sure, thanks." We did a little switch. Our backs were still facing each other but they were now touching. I heard him yawn. I yawned back in a show of camaraderie. Suddenly I could barely remember what we had been fighting about, and suddenly whatever it was didn't really matter. I was glad we weren't going to break that old marriage law; I knew our fight was now over and the anger was all gone. And I knew that whoever fell asleep second, which would probably be me, but maybe not because I was really super sleepy, would eventually flip to his or her other side and would snuggle in closer to the other. If it was me, I would find that place at the upper curve of his belly where my arm seemed to fit perfectly. If it was him, he would do that thing where he wrapped his arm all the way around me and pulled me in those last few centimeters so we were as close as possible. (I called this move the Lego because it reminded me of when you snapped two Lego pieces together with a snap that bonded them even tighter than two spoons.) I guess it didn't matter, I'd be happy either way.

CHAPTER THREE

For Richer
or Poorer

CAR KARMA

Studies show that there is something about being in a car that can upset even the most well-balanced relationships. (Okay, so these weren't the studies conducted in universities, more like the ones conducted over brunch with your girlfriends.) There are a lot of theories floating about regarding why this is so. Perhaps there is tension resulting from the ever-present possibility of having an accident and getting maimed or, even worse, dying. I couldn't even begin to count the number of times I had to assume crash position (throwing my arms in front of my face to shield it from flying glass) when in the car with Cosmas. Or perhaps it was because being confined in a fairly small space facing forward as opposed to toward each other made normal communication seem unnatural. In my particular case it was probably due to the fact that Cosmas and I each think the other is the worst driver ever. Also, I think that maybe men are just totally irrational when it comes to the car. And as everyone knows, in the fight of irrational versus rational, the irrational person always wins; you just cannot reason with someone who is irrational. Wasn't that the point?

I get accused of being hypersensitive (translation: thoughtful) and irrational (translation: creative) a lot by my husband, and maybe this is true, but I can remember only one instance when I was irrational in the car, and

A drugstore lipstick?! Did he know me at all?

I'm not sure the car had that much of a role in the situation. It was a weekend trip on which I asked Cosmas to turn around and drive thirty minutes back into the city to retrieve my forgotten makeup bag. His argument was that we were taking a weekend to get back to nature and that the chipmunks would not think less of me if I wasn't wearing makeup. I carefully explained that I could certainly go without makeup for a weekend, but that I had never gone more than twelve hours in my life (after age fifteen) without lipstick. He told me that I could buy some at the local drugstore when we got to our destination. A drugstore lipstick?! Did he know me at all? I told him our weekend away could very well be ruined. He asked me if this was a threat. I said only if it would work. He told me that it made absolutely no sense to lose over an hour of travel time over a dumb lipstick and that I was being completely irrational. I told him that I was well aware of the fact that I was being irrational but that I couldn't help it. He said that I made no sense because if I was rational enough to know that I was being irrational, then I should be rational enough to forget about the lipstick. I told him that the irrational side of me was winning. He told me not to give in. I begged and I pleaded, and eventually I wore him down.

We lost an hour and a half of drive time, got caught in traffic, got lost (which was not my lipstick's fault), and managed to just miss dinner at the bed and breakfast. Oops.

But this little squabble was nothing compared to the height of Cosmas's irrationality in car situations. Let me preface this by saying that our car trouble came out of nowhere; before we were married, I don't remember our ever having problems regarding the car. In fact, Cosmas was the only one of all the guys I dated who was able to teach me how to parallel park. (I learned to drive in Tennessee, where there are big parking lots and no need for such a skill.) This was no small feat as hundreds tried before him—okay not hundreds, but at least ten others before him had all failed. I consider myself to be an excellent driver, except when going in reverse. When I have to back up, I suddenly transform into a lousy driver. I have self-diagnosed my problem as reverse dyslexia, which means when in reverse I can never figure out which way to turn the wheel to go the direction that I want to go in.

Needless to say, my reverse dyslexia made parallel parking challenging. In addition to parallel parking together, we, well, parked. I remember one steamy-windowed night in a parking lot at the Westport train station that was certainly a positive experience. So I found it peculiar that our great car karma suddenly went bad after we got married.

Our first apartment in Boston did not have a parking space, so you either had to find street parking or you had to rent space in a garage. Since Cosmas had to work crazy hours and was often very tired, I didn't want him to have to hunt around for a space on the street, so I rented a space in the closest parking garage, which happened to be an eight-minute walk from the apartment. I didn't use the car much, so I didn't know we had a problem until one night when Cosmas picked me up from work.

We were almost home when I realized he had driven right past the garage, so I said, "Honey, you just passed the garage." He said that he wanted to see if he could find a street space closer to our apartment. I figured he was feeling particularly lazy and just didn't want to walk the eight minutes, and, in fact, I was feeling the same way, so at the time I agreed that it wouldn't hurt to check to see if there was anything closer. I thought he would drive down our street once or twice looking for a space and, if there wasn't one, would just go park in the garage. I thought wrong; instead, he started circling through the surrounding streets as well. Ten minutes passed and there were no spaces to be found; yet still he did not call it quits and head to the garage. Finally, I said, "Honey, I don't think there are any spaces close to home, so maybe we should just park in the garage." This was met with steely silence as again and again we looped around. I checked my watch; we had now been looking for parking for twenty minutes. So I said, "Honey, we've been looking for parking for the last twenty minutes; in the same time we could have parked at the garage and walked home by now."

He ignored me and we continued to circle around. Finally, I asked, "Is there some sort of primitive man-as-hunter thing going on here?" He gave me a derisive glance and at the next loop he pulled in front of our apartment and told me I should go on up to the apartment. At this point, I was truly perplexed. I needed answers. I asked why he didn't just go park in the garage.

The expression on his face convinced me it was best to get out of the car and go upstairs. From the front window in our apartment I could see the street below, and for the next half hour I saw him pass by every five minutes or so. When he finally came up, he didn't say a word about it, just sat on the couch and flipped on the TV. His mood appeared to be completely normal at this point, and he even patted the couch next to him. I approached him very cautiously, the way you would a strange dog you feared might be rabid, and tentatively sat down next to him. I tried to watch TV but wasn't able to concentrate so I grabbed the remote, turned off the TV, and asked, "Can we please talk about this?"

He responded with a completely innocent face. "Talk about what? Is something wrong?" I gestured toward the window and said, "The car, what was going on out there?" He just shrugged and said that he finally found a really great space on the street next to ours. I tried the friendly approach and asked him what made the space so great, and he said that it was right next to the side alleyway, so it was as close to our apartment as you could get without being on our street. I nodded as if I understood this, and then I asked him why he didn't want to park in the garage. Again, he shrugged and said that he preferred to park closer to the apartment. Not able to let it go, I pointed out that he actually spent forty-five minutes circling our neighborhood to find a space when it would have taken less then ten minutes to park in the garage and walk home. He responded by telling me that sometimes he finds a

Apparently he had a whole system worked out. I was dumbfounded. The whole thing made absolutely no sense whatsoever.

space almost immediately. I pressed him further and learned that once or twice he spent more than an hour and a half looking for a space.

Then he confessed that sometimes he double parks in front of our apartment and just waits for a car to leave. Apparently he had a whole system worked out. I was dumbfounded. The whole thing made absolutely no sense whatsoever. Who would circle around for an hour when there was an available space eight minutes away? I braced myself and asked him whether he had ever parked in the garage. He tried to dodge the question, but I would not be deterred. I told him I could go and find out. This made him all stony-faced because he really hated when I made threats. He calmly told me he had parked there maybe once or twice.

What this meant was that I had been paying $120 a month for the last three months *for nothing*. What a huge waste of money—we're talking two pairs of shoes or one pair of boots. *And* I started thinking back to all those times when he called to say that he was leaving work but then arrived home much later than the twenty minutes it should have taken for him to get home. So while I was starving and waiting to eat dinner, he was probably just circling around the neighborhood looking for parking. I was not amused.

I started riding home from work with him more often, just so I could get a better handle on the whole situation. It was actually worse than I thought; not only had he lost all reason when it came to parking, he apparently had lost his manners as well. It was as if he became an entirely different person—the change in personality was remarkable. Cosmas is extremely mild-mannered and always very amiable, which is not to say that he never gets angry, but it takes something significant to get him going. Well, apparently parking the car is one of those things. We'd be in the car having a perfectly nice conversation about our respective days, and as we got closer to home, he'd start to grow quiet. Even his body language shifted: I noticed that he'd begin to grip the steering wheel a little tighter; his eyes would narrow and dart back and forth; and he'd hunch over the wheel a bit, as if preparing to pounce. It was like watching a *National Geographic* special on wild animals hunting for prey.

The worst-case scenario was if we happened to be behind another car when a space opened up and the car in front of us took it. This drove Cosmas absolutely crazy with frustration. First he'd yell and swear at the car that left the space, but that was nothing compared to what he unleashed on the car that took the space. It wasn't as if the guy in front of us had stolen something that was rightfully ours.

When I pointed this out, Cosmas accused me of taking the other guy's side and told me that I wasn't being supportive. Never one to like accusations, I accused him of being deranged and asked him how I should have shown my support. Should I have gotten out of the car and charged at the guy who was taking the space that was rightfully his and pound on his window? Did he want me to sneak back later and maybe key the guy's car or slash his tires? We'd go round and round some more (bickering and driving) and finally he would drop me off at our apartment and I'd take a seat on our stoop to watch and wait.

Time and time again this same situation would

replay. Was parking the one part of his life he felt he could control? Or was this his way of venting—holding in all his frustrations and anger until he had a chance to redirect it toward something else, like the guy in the car in front of him who had just gotten a space?

I realized there on the stoop, watching Cosmas circle the block for the fifth time one night, that my husband's soul held mysteries that I would never unlock. Just as I will never know why they never give away a good color of lipstick in those free-gift-with-purchase bags, I will probably never understand why his showers take four times longer than mine, why he will use only the white Dove soap and not the pink Dove soap, why he refuses to change even one of his many, many P.I.N. codes or email passwords to my name, even when I beg and plead (this may fall into the "mean" category as opposed to the "irrational"), why he always says he is going to order the fish or the vegetarian plate but invariably orders red meat or the most cholesterol-laden dish on the menu when the waiter arrives, why he answers the phone when he knows it's me calling to make sure he's left already, and why he always whines about wanting more sweaters when no matter how many you buy him he will only wear the favorite sweater that he has named Baby Blue.

PLEASE THANK SLAVIA DOOITALL

It is a truth universally acknowledged by doctors' wives that however brilliant their husbands may be in the operating room, hospital, or laboratory, such aptitude quickly turns to ineptitude at home. I found this out one Thursday night after surviving another of my husband's drug dinners. I know that term must bring to mind all sorts of interesting images, but, trust me, it wasn't what you may think, not even close.

Pharmaceutical companies have *tons* of money, and in order to keep the money rolling in, they have to suck up to doctors who will prescribe their name-brand medications to their patients. So they invite young doctors to fancy restaurants in which they couldn't otherwise afford to dine, feed them well, offer free liquor, and then send them home with logo-bearing pens so they'll keep their now-favorite new stomach ulcer "drug of choice" in mind. Just to give you a taste, my very first foray into this glamorous world featured a world-renowned doctor giving a lecture at the table on how to extract foreign objects from the rectum. Bon appetit!

Anyway, after one such dinner, several of the doctors and their bored spouses ended up hanging out at the bar (big pharma kept the tab running), chatting away. After a long discussion about who was staying at what hotel for the upcoming Digestive Disease Week conference (fifty thousand gastroenterologists descending on some poor unsuspecting city for five days, can you imagine?) somehow the topic of conversation turned to the pagers the hospital issued, and what each doctor had picked as his "beep setting of choice"—riveting conversation, huh? So then one doctor casually mentioned that he was in need of a new battery yet again, and said that he wished batteries lasted longer. My husband, who tends not to participate in this kind of banal chitchat, then said, "Perhaps you're using cheap batteries, because my pager has used the same battery for the past eighteen months." These words, of course, caused a huge ruckus in this wild and crazy crowd. No one could believe it, because they all had to replace their batteries at least once every other month. But bless his heart, he stuck to his guns and told them that they must be buying dud batteries, because he had never (not even once) had to change his. He proudly passed around his pager for inspection, and, sure enough, the little battery symbol was brightly flashing its full wattage.

Leave it to another wife to solve the mystery. Mrs. Kayson looked right at him and said, "Maybe Jenny has been changing your batteries for you." Suddenly the whole table turned to face me. Taken totally off guard,

I just smiled and meekly raised my right hand. "Guilty as charged." Cosmas's facial expression was now frozen with horror and disbelief. He was mortified. Later in the car on the way home, he was pissed.

"How could you do that to me?" he demanded, his hands clenched the steering wheel, his knuckles white. "They laughed for ten minutes straight."

Now I was furious. "How could I do what to you? You're kidding, right? You're mad at me for being nice enough to change the batteries on your pager. I mean, hello, if your pager fails to go off because of a dead battery, people could die. I was trying to do my part in helping you save lives!"

He clicked off the radio. "How come I never saw you do it? I don't know if I believe you."

I tried to let that one go; it was late, and I was going to chalk it up to his bruised ego and late-night stupidity. The guy went to MIT for Christ's sake—shouldn't he know that batteries don't last forever?

But, like the Energizer Bunny, he kept going. "When exactly was the last time you supposedly changed the battery, and where did you buy the batteries that you used?"

WAS HE INSANE? WHAT WAS HE DOING? WAS HE TRYING TO CATCH ME IN SOME SORT OF LIE? No more *NYPD Blue* for him.

All bets were now off. "Actually, honey, you're right, it wasn't me. It was Slavia Dooitall, our maid. I'm surprised you've never run into her at the apartment. She's the one who always happens to notice that your pager is low on juice and buys batteries at these places called *grocery stores*—where they sell things like the *toothpaste* and the *Dove soap* that's ever present in the bathroom cabinet. She's the one who fills up the ice-cube trays. She's the one who washes the clothes all the time, so you never reach into your top drawer to find it devoid of boxer shorts! SHE'S THE ONE WHO PICKS YOUR SHIRTS UP OFF THE FLOOR, TAKES OUT THE COLLAR STAYS, TAKES THEM TO THE CLEANER, PICKS THEM UP, PUTS THE FREAKIN' COLLAR STAYS BACK IN, AND PUTS THEM BACK IN YOUR CLOSET! I MEAN, IF YOU'RE NOT DOING ANY OF THESE THINGS, AND I'M NOT DOING ANY OF THESE THINGS, THEN IT MUST BE THE MAID, RIGHT?!"

With that, I clicked the radio back on, and Tina Turner filled the car.

We arrived home and got ready for bed in total silence. It's quiet. It's dark. Moments slipped by, and finally I unclenched my fists and was just about to fall asleep.

Then, out of nowhere, he whispered, "So what did you say her name was?"

"Whose name?"

"Our housekeeper's name."

I smiled, despite the fact that I was still pissed. "Slavia Dooitall," I said, secretly patting myself on the back for extracting such a creative name out of my rectum (maybe I have managed to pick up a thing or two at these dinners after all).

"Well, please let her know that I'm very grateful for everything she does to make my life better. I hope she knows I'm sorry for taking her for granted."

A Rich Perspective on Being Poor

Most of my acquaintances believe that whoever is better at dealing with money should be the one in charge of the household finances. Every time I hear this wisdom I just nod and smile and say something like "Absolutely" or "You are so right." But what I'm thinking and what I want to ask is, "What if neither of us is good at the financial stuff?" or "Pray tell, how do we figure out who's better at such things?"

Cosmas and I were running a pretty tight race when it came to being irresponsible about money matters. I never opened my bank statements. (I used to throw them away unopened, but my mom found out and yelled at me, so now I throw them in a drawer.) I don't have an IRA or a 401(k), and I've never really been able to stick to a budget. My philosophy has never been one of moderation, and in the early years right after college I was quite famous for being really fun and extravagant at the beginning of each month; then I'd drop off the face of the earth for the last week or two, mainly because I was stone broke. I didn't mind, though, because I'd rather live really well, even for only half the time. In fact, right before we were married, I made a last-hurrah-before-getting-married purchase (via credit card) of a stunning red-dyed Persian lamb's wool coat with a beaver fur collar that was 75 percent off at Saks Fur Salon but still crazy expensive. (When Cosmas found out, it almost became my last-hurrah-before-untimely-death purchase.)

I've never really been able to stick to a budget.

Cosmas, on the other hand, had developed a false sense of financial security strictly because he had been a student forever and happened to be blessed with generous parents. So he didn't have to deal with paying rent, insurance, or making car payments until he was out of med school and started earning money on his own, which meant he had no idea how much things really cost (well, aside from a nice dinner or fancy cocktail at a chichi bar). He, too, had no savings account, never opened his bank statements, and never really managed to pay his bills on time. It was a match made in heaven.

When it came to figuring out who was best suited to handling our joint finances, it was pretty much a toss-up. We settled it by playing rock-paper-scissors, best three out of five. I lost, and I did not do it graciously. In fact, I still sometimes chastise myself over the final fateful round. I knew I should've gone rock over paper, but he had just done a scissors in round two and I assumed that Cosmas was not crafty enough to double-back two scissors in a row. (When I asked him about his strategy later, he just shrugged and said, "What strategy?" So annoying.)

I begged for a rematch decision with a game of Othello, double or nothing, where, if I lost, I'd throw in ten ten-minute back-scratch passes and five backrubs. He wanted us to play Yahtzee and demanded that I also throw in two weeks during which I would have to take out the trash. Looking back, I probably should have taken that deal; my record for beating him at Yahtzee was roughly fifty-fifty (he had the uncanny ability to always always get a Yahtzee, but if I got one, too, then I could usually beat him). But I passed on the deal he proposed because I thought he was being too greedy.

I countered with two out of three at backgammon, three days during which I'd take out the trash, and five backrubs. He pointed out the fact that he hadn't beaten me in backgammon in more than two years, and he offered up two out of three in Yahtzee and three weeks of my taking out the trash. I said no way and asked him where he learned to negotiate because you're not supposed to demand more on the second round. I also called him a big meanie and walked out of the room to flop down on our bed and pout. This was when he relented (I knew he would, because even when he's a big meanie, he's still a big softie) and agreed to another match of rock-paper-scissors, and I said fine, but insisted on making it best of five out of seven. I won the first three; he won the next two; I won game six, and he won the last three in a row by throwing the rock all three times.

As I had lost the second match fair and square (though I rue the fact that I had said best of seven, because I would have won best of five), I accepted that I was now in charge of dealing with money matters.

WE SLOWLY BECAME MORE FISCALLY RESPONSIBLE. A few of our friends already owned apartments or houses, and some were even talking about school districts for future children, and we both realized that if we ever wanted to buy our own apartment or house, we would have to pay down our debt, pay all our bills on time, spiff up our credit reports, and—duh—save some money. We cut up most of our credit cards, keeping only four that were to be used only in case of emergency. (I learned the hard way that Cosmas does not consider a Neiman Marcus last-call shoe sale an emergency.) We made a pact that we would use cash for everything.

It wasn't long before we found ourselves at the ATM on a Friday night, with no money in our account. I must have miscalculated somewhere along the line. Whoops. I was about to take a cash advance using a credit card, but Cosmas reminded me of our cash-only pact. I gave him a quizzical look and reminded him that we had seventeen dollars in our checking account for the next four days and that unless we could find an ATM that dispensed ten-dollar bills, we had no cash at all. He pulled me outside, away from the line that was gathering behind us, to discuss the matter. It was here that he told me he was sure we could both survive a few days with very little cash. I agreed that we "could" and countered with "But why would we want to?" I promised him that any money we took out on credit I'd replace the very next week.

Then he asked me if I remembered the movie *The Firm* with Tom Cruise. I said yeah and wondered where he was going with this. He told me that he always thought it was romantic when Mitch and Abby McDeere remembered their days of being newly married and poor. How they searched for money in the couch and saved up their pennies in a beer mug to buy a Chinese take-out dinner once a month. I then reminded him how Tom's character had also cheated on his wife with some floozy on the beach and asked him if he had something to tell me. He ignored my remark and explained once again that he thought it would be romantic if we spent the weekend poor and that maybe we'd appreciate even more what we had.

He thought it would be romantic if we spent the weekend poor.

I agreed on the condition that if we were going to do this, then we had to go all the way. There would be no backing out on Sunday when the whole experiment seemed more wretched than romantic. We shook on it and then went through our pockets to figure out how much money we had between us. I had $2.13, and he had $5.

I will admit that it was pretty fun in the beginning. We dropped our plans for getting Chinese and walked over to the local pizza shop. We had enough for one spaghetti and meatball dinner, which came with garlic bread and small salad ($5.50), and then we debated over getting two cans of soda or getting a plain cheese slice and just drinking water. We opted for one soda and decided we would buy and split a candy bar on the way home. It was like the famous scene from *Lady and the Tramp* as we stared all goo-goo-eyed at each other and laughed a great deal over our small dinner. We savored every bite and soaked up every last bit of sauce with the bread. We discussed how much cash we thought we could round up for the rest of the weekend. Cosmas knew there was at least three dollars in change in the car. I was positive that if I went through my various purses I'd find some misplaced cash. We also had a coffee can full of change that we could trade in at the local supermarket in one of those change machines. I told him that we really had very little food at home as I hadn't gone grocery shopping in a while. I knew there were some frozen vegetables in the freezer and some cans in the cupboards and maybe a frozen pizza or two, but little else. He reassured me that we'd be fine and gallantly offered that I be the one to pick out the candy bar to split. I ended up picking a Kit Kat, hoping that by breaking it into four bars we would feel as if we had more than we actually did.

When we got home, we immediately tore our apartment apart looking for cash. Cosmas went hunting for change and began making stacks of quarters, dimes, nickels, and pennies on the kitchen table while I methodically went through every purse and pocket in the house. Every time I found anything, whether it was a dime or a few crumpled dollar bills, I screamed out with glee. When I found a twenty stashed in the pocket of my Walkman carrying case (a cash reserve in case I jog too far and need to take a cab home), we actually danced around the living room for a while and Cosmas told me that he was almost up to $30 in change. In no time we became overconfident and started saying things like, "What were we worried about?" "Money, we have tons of it." "This is going to be cake." At the end of the night we ended up with $31.22 in change (they took 2 percent of the total when we went to cash it in at ten o'clock) and $36 in bills. We decided to leave the change in the car as an emergency stash. With almost $68 we felt rich, and since we had shared such a paltry dinner we were starving, so we stopped by our favorite ice-cream place and each got a cone (at $3.25 each, we had $60.72 remaining).

Despite the ice cream we both woke up starving the next morning and went out and bought eggs, bagels, a small container of cream cheese, bacon, and orange juice. We split a large Starbucks coffee (total cost was $17.77, but we said that would partially cover two more breakfasts, so we had $42.95 remaining). We went to a matinee and ordered a medium popcorn and drink instead of the large. (I was going to get a small, but I fell for the quarter more to upgrade one size. I actually felt a twinge of guilt over my decision, but I reasoned that we were already forgoing our standard Snow Caps. I mean, were we to live like savages?) This left us with a total of $21.45 remaining by five P.M. of day two. On the way home we picked up a two-cheeseburger supersize combo at McDonald's and decided we'd have it with soup at home (it was $4.23, so we had $17.22 remaining). In less than twenty-four hours we had gone from close to seventy dollars to less than twenty. So much for being rich.

On Sunday, we played it lean and mean. We had eggs and bacon, and since we didn't have any bread I made some baked beans for our morning carb. I wasn't worried about our expenses for the day because I usually spend every Sunday reading the *New York Times* and finishing any magazines that I had left over from the week; Cosmas was planning on going to work for the day.

Disaster struck moments later when I went down to get the paper and it wasn't there. This would irritate me on a normal day—either someone had stolen it or there had been a mixup with my delivery, but today it caused me something close to panic. I raced up the stairs and began frantically looking around for an old paper so that I could call for a redelivery. Where were all the papers? Normally we have a huge stack by the door that just grows and grows since neither of us wants to take it down to recycling. Time was of great importance, because they can redeliver only if you call by a certain time; otherwise they just credit your account. I bellowed to Cosmas and asked him what had happened to all the papers; he looked at me a bit queerly and reminded me that I had made him take them down to recycling that morning while I was making

Disaster struck moments later when I went down to get the paper and it wasn't there.

breakfast. I grabbed the phone, dialed information, got the number, and called. I was informed by a soothing yet cheerful automated voice that they were so very sorry I did not receive my paper, they were even sorrier that it was too late for redelivery, and that they were going to credit my account $3.75. The voice then instructed me to have a nice day.

Crushed, I looked up to see Cosmas standing in the doorway of our bedroom, smart enough to watch from a distance. I told him that my paper wasn't downstairs and then asked him if he saw it when he was throwing out the papers. He shook his head, said he wasn't sure, and looked down at the floor; we both realized that if he had noticed then, it would have been in time for redelivery. I stared him straight in the eye and said, "I have to get a *Sunday Times*. I need the *Sunday Times*." He asked how much it cost, and I glumly told him $3.50, which seemed like a gigantic amount considering we had less than twenty bucks to make it through today and tomorrow. I knew that I should be able to forgo it for one lousy week when the money should go toward something else—like food. One option would be that I could go to Starbucks where they always put out one free paper for customers, but that was a sport where you had to be aggressive in trying to find all the sections and asking strangers whether you could have next dibs on the section they were currently reading. I shuddered just thinking about it; besides if I went, I'd have to buy a cup of coffee and that's the same price as a paper. And I happened to be fairly obsessive-compulsive in terms of how I liked to read the paper Book Review, Styles front-page stories only, Magazine, rest of Styles, Maureen Dowd's column in the Week in Review, Business, Front Page, and I'd end by looking at the pictures in the Travel section. If I didn't read the paper, what would I do all day? I told Cosmas that I was more than willing to forgo a meal in the next day or two for the paper.

He agreed and even offered to go get it. This was strange, because he had yet to shower, and Cosmas goes nowhere without showering first. He's done it only once when we didn't have any hot water or electricity during a snowstorm and I had insisted that we walk to the local hardware store for a flashlight and candles. I didn't question him about his intentions because I didn't want to lose the paper, but I did offer to go with him. He said it wasn't necessary. I said I knew that it wasn't necessary but that I wanted to go and stretch my legs. He said that he'd take a walk with me after he came back and took a shower. I told him that I'd be reading the paper for the rest of the morning and that I'd walk with him before dinner, but that I still wanted to go with him now. He gave me a pout and said something so softly I couldn't even hear him. So I said, "What?" Reluctantly, he said it again, a little louder this time: "Bread."

"Excuse me?" I asked. "Bread? What are you talking about?" He mumbled that he wanted to buy some bread, that breakfast wasn't breakfast without it—toast, bagel, croissant, or English muffin—and he explained that it was a Greek thing. Delighted that he, too, had his weakness, I said no problem. Besides, bread was cheap. Soon I was off to the store by myself, and I bought a paper, a croissant, a bagel, and two individually wrapped Swedish fish candies ($5.20; we now had $12.02 remaining). I hummed as I walked home, and I heard Cosmas humming in the shower when I got back. Everybody was happy.

Lunch consisted of frozen French bread pizza for me (Cosmas munched his bread), cream of mushroom soup, and water. Afterward, Cosmas left for work with a dollar in his pocket for a Diet Coke; to be fair I allocated myself some Diet Coke money as well. We now had ten bucks. We had discussed meeting for dinner around eightish, and I told him that all we had was a bag of peas, more mushroom soup, a sleeve of Fig Newtons, one packet of microwave popcorn that I thought was over a year old, and some crackers that were probably stale. Cosmas told me that the crackers were indeed stale (he ate them anyway) and there was now only half a sleeve of Fig Newtons.

That night we had peas and soup and were both hungry an hour later. Although we probably could have survived on the meager meal, all we could think about was more food. Cosmas pointed out every time his stomach growled, and my way of coping was to name foods that I would love to have—meat loaf and mashed potatoes, macaroni and cheese, California rolls, Kentucky Fried chicken, key lime pie . . . but Cosmas eventually made me stop. I suggested we take a walk to get our minds off of food, but he told me that by exercising we'd only work up more of an appetite (which was a lame way of saying he didn't want to go for a walk), so then I reminded him of the old packet of microwave popcorn. In the process of trying to get every single kernel to pop, it started to burn, and once we picked through it getting rid of the burned pieces, we had only a small handful left. Cosmas divided it up piece by piece, and we ate each piece with a slow deliberation, both claiming that we had never tasted popcorn so good. Afterward I suggested that we go to bed, because the sooner this day ended, the sooner tomorrow would come; by midnight tomorrow we would be flush again.

It's difficult to sleep when you're hungry, and we both tossed and turned. In the dark, watching Cosmas flip around, I realized how much he resembled a giant chili dog. Finally, at one in the morning we got in the car and drove to Store 24, where we proceeded to blow the last of our money on Gatorade, a large bag of pizza pretzel Combos, two frozen corn dogs, and a pint of Ben and Jerry's Bovinity Divinity. We inhaled the Combos in the car on the way home, raced each other up the stairs in anticipation of the corn dogs and Gatorade, then demolished them in less than sixty seconds. When all we had left was the ice cream, we crawled into bed and ate it very slowly, savoring each sweet bite. An hour later we fell asleep full (a little grossed out), contented, and stone broke.

In the dark, watching Cosmas flip around, I realized how much he resembled a giant chili dog.

The next morning was chaos since we both overslept and had to rush off before we even had a chance to discuss the fact that we had no money. I knew that Cosmas would be okay; there was always a free lunch to be had somewhere in the hospital, and even if he couldn't find any leftover sandwich platters from lunchtime conferences, there were always the cookies and juice boxes that were kept in the mini-fridge for the patients to have after undergoing colonoscopies.

But what about dinner? Hmmm, in the movies the place to get quick cash was from a pawnshop, but I wasn't sure how to find one and I didn't know what I would hock. I decided to sell one of my signed first edition books to a used bookstore. A Don DeLillo or a Margaret Atwood should bring in at least thirty or forty bucks, which we could blow on a big dinner. Meanwhile, Cosmas had the same idea, and he answered an ad that one of the labs at the hospital had posted. He spent his lunch hour giving a pint of blood, feeling faint, sitting with his head between his legs for the next forty-five minutes, and collecting $20 on his way out the door.

It wasn't exactly an O. Henry story, but it ended happily, with just as much love and $50 worth of sushi.

CHAPTER FOUR

In Sickness and Health

In Sickness . . . or Maybe Not

The first clue that I was sick was that my eyes were a bit crusty when I opened them; well, crustier than normal. I raised my head slightly so I could squint at the digital clock, and the sudden throbbing that ensued confirmed something was off. My throat was tight, my head felt a bit thick, and my nose was stuffed up. Drat. I must be sick. I had already learned that the joys of being sick—the ice-cream milk shakes, the pancake lunches, the "poor baby's"—are gone when you are no longer living at home with your mom. But I was lucky. I had traded up—I now shared a bed with someone who specialized in tending to the sick, so I figured this flu would be a cakewalk.

Cosmas was asleep with his back to me. I swallowed hard and tried to breathe into my nose as a final check to make sure I was really sick—affirmative. I then nudged him on the shoulder. No response. I nudged again and said, "Cosmas, wake up." Normally this would go on for a few minutes, but I figured these were extenuating circumstances, so I cut to the chase and shook him harder and said, "Cosmas, I'm sick." This got a response, probably because his doctor brain was now hardwired to respond to the word *sick,* but he didn't turn over or anything. He remained frozen, knowing that if he moved too much he would risk actually waking up his bladder. I got a muffled "What's wrong?" So I recounted my symptoms; when I finished he informed me that I was not sick, that I had a cold.

What if I was to take a turn for the worse? What if he came home to find me splayed out on the floor with the phone in my hand, having been too weak even to dial 911?

That's it? Was he some sort of magic doctor who was able to diagnose me while basically asleep? He didn't even look at me! Maybe it just sounded like a cold, but what if it wasn't? Or what if it was, but somewhere things go bad and I was to take a turn for the worse? This happened a lot in soap operas. What if he came home to find me splayed out on the floor with the phone in my hand, having been too weak even to dial 911? I reminded him of the very sad story he once told me of a fellow resident whose wife had the flu for two weeks and later ended up dying from it because she had an undiagnosed raging bacterial infection. Naturally, the husband could not forgive himself for letting her die. This worked, and he flipped over to face me. I snuffled a hello and tried to look as pitiful as possible.

He was all business though, well, as all business as a doctor could be lying in bed wearing only boxers. He felt my forehead, felt the glands alongside my neck, and made me say "Ahhh." This is when I nailed him. He had me going for a while, but now I knew it had all been window dressing. It was way too dark in the room for him to see the back of my throat, and he hadn't even put on his glasses; I could have purple spots all over me and he wouldn't have been able to see them. I pushed him away.

He pulled me into a hug and assured me that I was fine—I just had a little cold. He promised me that he would know if I were ever really sick, and that he would act accordingly if such a situation presented itself. Trust me, it's just a cold, he said one more time for emphasis, and with that he got out of bed and headed toward the bathroom. I called after him saying that I hoped he was right, for his sake. I eventually got out of bed myself. I knew he was right, but that wasn't the point. When it came right down to it, I certainly wasn't wishing for some raging illness, but what I wanted was a little bit of sympathy. Is a glass of orange juice and a pat on the head too much to ask for? I didn't even need the "poor baby."

By the time he left for work he knew that I was still a little bummed out because I'm normally pretty chatty in the morning. He called me his own personal morning show because I'd yammer on about the weather or whatever I had dreamed the night before, but this morning I was quiet except for the occasional blowing of the nose or clearing of the throat. When he came over to kiss me good-bye, he pressed his lips on my forehead and left them there for a moment longer than normal, and he looked down on me and said, "I think you have a fever." I looked up, suddenly smiling and feeling vindicated, "Really?" I asked. And he shook his head no and said that he was just joking. A little doctor humor, I suppose. Hardy har har.

Of course I ran into Mary Sunshine when I went down to get the newspaper, and she instantly picked up on the fact that I was sick and cooed a bit of sympathy at me. She then said what everyone always says, which was that it must be mighty nice to have a doctor for a husband on such occasions. I told her the opposite was the case, and I repeated the truism that a painter's house always needs painting. She was nice enough to give me a "poor baby" after I sneezed. I should have just said my good-bye at that point and gone on my sniffling way, but I was already feeling sorry for myself, so I thought I might as well ask what her perfect husband did when she was sick. She told me how he'd get her all set up in bed, hooking up the TV and VCR on their nightstand so she could watch movies; how he'd go out and buy oranges and squeeze her fresh orange juice, being careful to strain out the seeds; and how one time he went out and bought her favorite childhood book and read to her. Hmmm, I wondered whether Cosmas even knew my favorite childhood book—not likely. So of course this made me feel worse, and I just let out a big sigh, waved, and headed back to our apartment. She called after me that she'd make me some chicken soup, but I wouldn't get it until tomorrow because she needed a day to make the broth.

My cold held pretty steady for the next few days, but on Thursday I took a turn for the worse. I was coughing continually, and it wasn't a dry cough either. It was a rib-shaking, diaphragm-rattling, green-glob-upbringing sort of cough. I was up for most of the night and had tried once or twice to wake Cosmas, but to no avail. By morning I was tired, cranky, and totally fed up. So I did the grown-up thing and gave him the silent treatment. When he asked me how I was feeling, I snippily replied, "What's it to you?" He asked me again, and then I told him everything he had missed when he was sleeping. How I stubbed my toe on the way to make myself tea. How we didn't have any tea. How I heated up some lemonade and then I burned my tongue on it. How I had gone through half a box of Kleenex and my nose was now sore and raw, and then I opened up a used one to show him the green stuff—my evidence that this was no cold. I told him how I tried to wake him up but he wouldn't budge. I told him that I called my brother—who, conveniently, is also a doctor—at three A.M. and that he had sat on the phone with me for twenty minutes and listened to all my ailments, and that he thought perhaps I had an upper respiratory infection and maybe antibiotics would make me feel better. I then asked whether he could write me a prescription for antibiotics.

Now the only thing Cosmas hated more than my calling my brother for a second opinion was when I took my brother's opinion over his. In a very defensive tone, he said it was probably hard for my brother truly to assess my current illness over the phone, and my retort was that he probably learned the method at the same place where

Cosmas had learned to diagnose me with his back turned toward me. He rolled his eyes and told me that he was sticking by his assessment that I had a cold, and that while, yes, green stuff did normally indicate a possible infection, it was probably viral, meaning antibiotics wouldn't help. I would simply have to let it run its course. He said he was against wantonly prescribing antibiotics and explained that it was easy to build up a tolerance, which wouldn't be good when I really needed them.

I had been cutting a lemon to put in my hot water (no tea, remember?) during this symposium on the misuse of antibiotics, and I finally had it with his lack of sympathy. Just as I was about to tell him that I couldn't give a rat's ass about whether or not I had a cold or was dying from scarlet fever, that all I wanted was for him to show a little concern for me, I cut my fin-

He stared at the bloody towel, looked up at me, and then slumped to the floor.

ger. When I whipped around to yell at him, the blood from my new cut slapped him in the face. He recoiled and wiped his face; as he was looking down at the blood on his hands, I suddenly felt the pain of the cut as well as the lemon juice that was now in it. I heard screaming, and at first I assumed it was me, since I was the one who had the cut, but as I grabbed a kitchen towel to press onto my wound, I realized it wasn't me who was screaming, it was Cosmas. Alarmed by this realization, I turned around once again. He stared at the bloody towel, looked up at me, and then slumped to the floor. I stood there for a second, not really sure what had just happened. This is when I checked to make sure I still had a finger left; I did. The cut was long but not particularly deep.

So I crouched on the floor to see what had happened with Cosmas, and I was suddenly all panicky. What just happened? Did he pass out? Did he have a heart attack? Stroke? Aneurysm? Blood clot to the brain? (The downside of knowing so many doctors is that I have a pretty good inventory of things that can drop a person in his tracks.) I bent over him, and he seemed to be breathing okay; he wasn't turning blue or anything. I jumped up, grabbed the phone, threw open the fridge, pulled out a pitcher of lemonade, and started pouring it on his face. . . . Isn't that what they do in the movies to wake someone up? If he didn't instantly respond, I was ready to call 911.

He sat straight up sputtering, and I screamed, which made him scream, which made me scream again. By this time there was a banging on the door. It was Mary, asking whether everything was all right. I opened the door, and she shrieked when she saw the bloody towel in my hand, then screamed again when she saw Cosmas on the floor with the bloody knife right next to him. And she screamed as I dragged her inside and slammed the door behind her. I must admit that I somewhat took advantage of the current situation and said what I'd been dying to say to Mrs. Mary Sunshine for so long, "MARY, SHUT THE HELL UP! EVERYTHING IS FINE!" I paused, looking down at Cosmas who was still on the floor sputtering out the lemonade that had gone up his nose, and continued, "I think." Which is when I turned to Cosmas and said, "What the hell was that, did you faint?"

Cosmas just sat there running his fingers through his now wet hair, and he sort of shrugged bashfully. Mary pulled away the towel to inspect my finger, and as she did so I saw Cosmas's eyes go a little wild, and he looked as if he was about to faint again. I considered going over to him to do my Cher imitation from *Moonstruck*, slapping him and telling him to snap out of it; instead, I stomped my foot and shouted, "DON'T FAINT. I'M FINE," which seemed to work just as well.

So it turned out that my brilliant doctor husband apparently faints at the sight of his own blood, and now he faints at the sight of mine, too. In fact, that time that he gave blood for money at the hospital, he hadn't just felt faint, he had actually fainted. He woke up on a gurney an hour later. I had mixed feelings about this. In some ways, wasn't one of the perks of being married to a doctor having on-hand medical care in case of an accident? What good would it do me if he fainted if I ever got really hurt? Then I realized Mary was yammering on and on about something. Oh well, her silence had been too good to be true anyway, and as I tuned her back in, I realized she was drawling in her melodious voice "Ooooh, I think it's just darlin' that he fainted; it's romantic Cosmas showing you how much he loves you. He just got so worked up about the thought of you bein' really hurt, not just on an emotional level but on a physiological one as well." Interesting, now we're getting somewhere.

Soon we were all drinking tea (Mary had gone to get her tea box . . . she had twenty-four different kinds to select from, a few she had made herself, having learned the art of the tea ceremony on a recent trip to Japan). Mary and I had decided that my cut wasn't worth stitches, and together we bandaged it up with gauze and tape. Cosmas just sat quietly and drank his tea and slowly ate his piece of cranapple loaf. (She bakes fresh breakfast bread every morning for her hubby's breakfast. Don't we all?) He averted his eyes from me as I kept asking if he was okay. He nodded that he was fine and finally murmured that he was a bit embarrassed by what had happened.

Mary promptly held up three fingers and swore she'd never tell (4-H honor). I'm not sure if he was talking to himself or to us, but he said that he had seen some incredibly gruesome things during his rotations through the hospital, people who have cut entire limbs off (ugh) and people who had been in fires, and that it had never bothered him before, but that when he saw me with blood all over my hands, he just seized up, suddenly terrified that I might be hurt, and then, whammo. I told him not to worry about it, that with me I guess he was more of a husband than a doctor.

I decided to side with Mary on this one and view the whole situation as very romantic. Maybe he wasn't the greatest at handling colds, but I knew when it came to the big stuff he'd be there for me—well, at least be lying on the floor near me, and that's basically all I really wanted anyway.

ALL HAIL THE DINNER DICTATOR

There are many different kinds of ruts you fall into during your life. There's the career rut, the workout rut, the what-should-I-do-with-my-hair rut, and the ice-cream rut (not all ruts have to be bad, mind you). I've been in all of them and have always somehow managed to pull myself out. So I guess it's logical that when you're married, a whole new menu of possible ruts opens up and then you fall into one together, like the how-come-we-always-rent-two-movies-on-Friday-and-watch-one-on-Friday-night-and-one-on-Saturday-night-and-never-do-anything-exciting rut, the fine-if-you-want-fun-then-let's-go-to-a-Saturday-matinee-movie rut, and the if-you-think-seeing-a-Saturday-movie-at-the-theater-instead-of-on-the-couch-qualifies-as-fun-and-exciting-then-you've-got-a-lot-to-learn rut.

I do think couple ruts are much harder to escape because it takes the will and determination of both people, and during the struggle to get out sometimes you only get yourself in deeper. This is what happened to us; we had fallen into what I think is the most horrible rut of them all, the dreaded what-should-we-do-for-dinner? rut. In fact, we've been flailing about in this rut for so long it has become a very deep ditch, yes, the dreaded deep dinner ditch.

I must admit that I was a bit naive when it came to the importance of food in a marriage. Since eating is one of life's most basic tasks and both of us had managed to subsist on our own before we got married, I just assumed that it would be an easy transition to marriage—meaning, I thought everything would be the same. Cosmas and I have always been vastly different when it comes to our attitude and our tastes in food, but it never really seemed to be an issue, well, at least not to me. He loves French food, pâté, exotic meats, bitter greens, and he'll even eat liver. So when we go to French restaurants, I order a steak frites and try not to gag at the site of his eating snails on toast. The one time I asked him for one of his escargots he was thrilled, but his excitement quickly turned to dismay as he watched me plop the sucker onto my bread plate and sprinkle it with salt to see if a cooked snail will shrivel the way a live one does (it doesn't), and said that I was worse than a small child when it comes to food (I am).

In some ways he was right; I have not managed to evolve that far in my tastes for food. Sure, I'll eat oysters and caviar, and I do enjoy sushi, but I also have a huge fondness for any food that's processed and bad for you. You know, those unnaturally red Twinkielike things with some random "cream" filling that you see in gas-station convenience stores and can't help but sort of stare at. Maybe if you're really brave you sort of poke at it and then pull back in horror as the wrapper becomes smudged with some oily substance. Then say, "Ugh, who eats these things? I bet they have the shelf life of like a thousand years." Well, case closed. It's me. I buy them. I eat them. I like them.

I also eat jelly doughnuts, Kraft Macaroni and Cheese, Pop-Tarts, Swedish fish candies, Chipwiches, and Stove Top stuffing. In fact, I've been known to eat many of the above items for dinner, singularly or in combination. One of my staple dinners when single involved opening up a can of SpaghettiOs, grabbing a spoon, and eating it straight from the can. Sometimes for a change of pace I'd put them in the fridge and eat them cold. Cosmas claims it's one of the grossest things he's ever seen, and I'm now banned from engaging in such activity when within twenty yards of him.

Well, my assumption of food status quo was wrong. As soon as we got back from the honeymoon, we were out at a very upscale Italian place where my order broke the camel's back. I asked if the kitchen could make me a plate of spaghetti and meatballs. The snotty waiter took my request only slightly better than Cosmas, whose eyes got huge and his hands went over his open mouth in sheer horror. The waiter gave me a little smirk of disgust and wouldn't even dignify my question with a response. I rolled my eyes and tried to laugh it off. Once the waiter left to go tell all the other waiters what the silly American woman tried to order at table 17 (hellooooo, this is America, it's a free country, y'know), Cosmas leaned in and gave me his best whispered shout, our candle flickering in the wake of the words he stressed. "Do you *think* we can start getting you to eat like a grown-up?"

I challenged back, "Perhaps we can when we start speaking to me like a grown-up. Please, plenty of grown-ups eat spaghetti and meatballs. I know for a fact that even the mafia eats spaghetti and meatballs, so why don't you go tell Michael Corleone that he should perhaps learn to eat in a more mature fashion. C'mon, I dare you."

He gave me the exasperated sigh and said in the most serious of tones, "You know very well this is not an issue of spaghetti and meatballs."

This, of course, caused me to break out into laughter; I did my best imitation of a stern Cosmas face and said, "You know very well this is not an issue of spaghetti and meatballs." Lucky for me, he cracked a smile and all was forgiven. But the incident, now fondly known as the Spaghetti and Meatball Summit, was the launching pad of a serious discussion about how we were going to handle food in our new marriage. I was surprised to learn that Cosmas really expected and wanted us to eat together whenever possible. He also outlined very specific guidelines to what he considered dinner, and most of my favorite snacks did not make the list.

I ended up giving in because I thought it was very sweet that he wanted to eat together, and deep down I knew my eating habits were rather atrocious. Great. Done. All was now decided.

So then he said, "You do know that we can't eat out and order takeout for the rest of our lives." This was his not-so-subtle segue into the touchy subject of cooking at home. He reminded me of the thousands of dollars in kitchen stuff that we had received as wedding presents (the majority of it coming from my in-laws). This caused me to undergo a flashback to my bridal shower, where I opened box after box of frying pans, saucepans, and pasta pans. I can still hear the voices rising above the oohs and ahhs, "Look, Jenny, it's a frying pan. You use a frying pan to cook things like eggs, and they won't stick to this pan because it's a *nonstick* frying pan. Since it's a *nonstick* frying pan, you have to use plastic utensils. So remember, use only plastic utensils on your new *nonstick* frying pan. You can't use metal ones." Did they think I grew up in a cave? Did they think I'm a moron? Who doesn't know what a frying pan looks like? Even when I used a frying pan to hammer a nail into my wall once I still knew that it was a frying pan. But I smiled and took it because it wasn't really the right time to explain the difference between not being able to cook and choosing not to cook. I would like to get a T-shirt printed that reads: IT'S NOT THAT I CAN'T COOK. I DON'T COOK.

Cosmas questioned this edict of mine. "So, why is it that you don't like to cook again? You know, I think cooking is fun." I was thinking that if he thinks it's so much fun, then he should do all the cooking, but I knew I would probably not win that battle either. I was desperate to end the S&M Summit, so I agreed that I would start to cook once in a while as long as he did as well.

We started off with a plan where two nights a week he'd cook, two nights a week I'd cook, and two nights we'd go out or do takeout. I insisted on at least one night of catch-as-catch-can, which meant that we were both left to fend for ourselves. He'd have to get his own dinner, and I, in turn, could do whatever I wanted with mine. Those were soon my favorite nights of the week.

Like a good sport, I really tried to make good on my side of the agreement, though I have to admit I took the easy way out. I started to look for meals that were contained in boxes. I made Rice-A-Roni dishes. I made Hamburger Helper. I made a Betty Crocker cake (though apparently this **No really, I've had good Hamburger Helper in my day, but this one is especially delicious.** didn't count, as it was not "proper" dinner food). I bought high-end frozen dinners. I grilled hot dogs on the George Foreman grill. I heated chicken nuggets

(I even mixed real honey with mustard for a homemade dipping sauce). We had Old El Paso Taco Night. We had Old El Paso Burrito Night. We had Old El Paso Fajita Night. I made a spinach lasagna. I made egg salad. I made a broccoli-and-rice casserole. In the beginning Cosmas went overboard praising whatever I made, "No really, I've had good Hamburger Helper in my day, but this one is especially delicious." So once I figured he liked something, I'd start making it over and over until we both hated it. What I didn't realize is that you constantly have to expand your repertoire of dinner menus at the same time as you rotate them so as not to cause burnout. Live and learn. We were officially in a dinner rut.

Cosmas worked us deeper into the rut with talk of all the fabulous things he was going to make that never seemed to materialize. He became a cook-tease. Instead of baked chicken and roasted rosemary potatoes, we had grilled cheese sandwiches. Instead of chili and hearty stews, he made a lot of salads. Instead of grilled Cajun shrimp and seared vegetable kabobs, he heated tomato sauce and boiled pasta.

Our schedule started to break down and after we reshuffled our household task list, Cosmas offered to be in charge of the grocery shopping. He went only once, and little by little our fridge became bare. Cooking is very similar to going to the gym: once you break from your schedule, it's hard to go back. So, soon, we were back to relying mainly on takeout, and we began to eat a lot of sandwiches.

But where we crossed the line of rutdom to ditchdom is that I got a bad case of DDDS, Dreaded Dinner Discussion Syndrome. Trying to figure out what, where, and when to eat was, in the beginning, seemingly benign chitchat between husband and wife, but after having the same discussion more than three hundred times, it started to wear on me. Another hundred times made me develop a slight facial tick. Another hundred times and I was done for.

When I was around six years old, I started to take violin lessons. Obviously the violin can make beautiful music, but in the beginning stages I think it's comparable to a screaming cat. What was even worse was all I knew how to play was "Twinkle, Twinkle, Little Star." Over and over. I remember my mother coming into the living room where I was practicing, her hands shaking. She said in a quiet voice that it was time to stop, and then she promptly called my teacher and told him that if he didn't teach me another song, he'd be sorry. Then she slammed down the phone and walked out of the room. I now understand what happened; she had just snapped.

I could now completely sympathize, and I squirmed just thinking about it. Cosmas always started the discussion. "So what do you think in terms of dinner?" Then I would say, "I dunno, what do you feel like having?" Then he'd say he didn't know and then I'd started naming things, Chinese, Thai, Indian, Mexican, pasta, etc., etc. Then we'd have to discuss each choice, No on Chinese, not in the mood. Thai is out because we had it last night. Maybe Mexican, but where should we go. Yadda yadda yadda.

I grew to despise the very thought of dinner. So one day I gave up. I knew I had crumbled when I refused to pick up the phone, knowing it was Cosmas calling to discuss you-know-what. I just sat there at the kitchen table and listened to his tinny voice come through the machine, "Honey? Honey, are you there?" Then I heard my cell phone start to ring, but I made no move to answer it. Then I heard the home phone ring again, and he said it into the machine, "Hello, it's me. I'm just calling to see what you want to do about dinn—" at which point I ran screaming from the room. Suddenly I whipped out the calculator and figured out that if both of us live to be eighty and we ate dinner together twenty-four nights a month, then we were faced with the overwhelming necessity of figuring out what we were going to have for dinner

FOURTEEN THOUSAND SIX HUNDRED AND FIFTY MORE TIMES! I almost fainted.

Later, when Cosmas walked in the door and said, "Where were you? I've been calling . . . ," I lifted my head up off the table where I had been resting it on the calculator, and indentations from the calculator keys were now pressed into my cheek. I raised my hand to stop him from speaking (it's surprisingly effective), and I said, "I am surrendering. I am officially declaring you the new dinner dictator of our marriage. There will be no more discussions, as this is no longer a democracy. I am hereby giving up all my voting rights. I give you unmitigated power of attorney to be solely in charge of my dinner welfare."

He responded in the way anyone would when talking to someone who has obviously snapped; it's sort of the same tone you would take when faced with a crazed psycho killer who's foaming at the mouth and wielding a very large machete—very calm, very quiet, about an octave lower than his normal voice. "Now honey, I think we're overreacting just a tiny bit when it comes to the subject of—"

I raised my hand again, "Please don't say it."

"Okay, I won't, but I don't think a dictatorship is going to solve the problem." So I told him that I thought it would. I told him I couldn't possibly deal with one more mundane discussion about what we were going to eat for dinner. I showed him my calculations—14,650 more dinners—and let out a small whimper. This sort of kicked him into action, and he took charge of the situation. He decided that having a dinner dictator every night might actually be a pretty good idea, but he didn't think it should only be him. He thought we should trade off. I suggested a four-year term of office, and he suggested switching week to week.

We decided that when it was your turn to be the dinner dictator, you truly had to make *all* the decisions. If you decided that we were going to eat out, then you had to pick the place. If you decided it was a good night for takeout, it was then up to you to pick the place, order the food, and pick it up. Same rules applied for cooking. That way the other person would have the luxury of not having to worry about what to do for dinner and could just live in peace knowing that at the end of the day he or she would be served a meal. Of course, there was the standard no-complaints clause for whoever was receiving the meal.

We had let dinner take over our lives when we were the ones who should have been in charge.

I know it may just seem like semantics, but there is a slight difference in its being your duty to cook dinner ("duty" implies chore) and your being solely and completely in charge of dinner ("in charge" implies power). Psychological empowerment and having a flashy title does wonders for the attitude, because when it was my turn to rule I took my job very seriously. Like any good dictator I wanted to be respected by my people (Cosmas), and to be respected I knew I had to lead. So I began to think about dinner in a whole new way. We had let dinner take over our lives when we were the ones who should have been in charge. Each week involved strategy and a plan for execution (I've seen a lot of war movies). I would sit down at the beginning of the week and map it all out ahead of time. I tried to think about what Cosmas would like for dinner and what I would like for dinner, and I figured out how much time I could give to the task at hand. Cosmas enjoyed his weeks as dictator, too, because he was finally able to get me into restaurants that I would never try before, and we began the arduous task of evolving my palette.

Our new dictatorship rules slowly but surely got us out of our ditch and to the point where we were just back into a rut. Now, as for getting us out of the rut—I knew that would probably take a bit more creative energy (or a personal chef), but I guess if you had to be stuck in one at all, it was better to be stuck in one together, right? Only 14,640 or so more to go.

THE FAT FILES

My mother broached the topic in her usual delicate manner; giving me her best dead-on stare, she said, "You're getting fat." This was where I normally flipped out, telling her that I hate the fact that she's always been hypercritical when it came to my weight and then I'd get in trouble for using that tone of voice with her, but not this time. This time I just meekly nodded and said, "You're right, Mom. I am."

She opened her mouth, ready to launch into the next step of her game plan, which was proving to me that I had gained weight by giving me a hand mirror so I could view my fat cheeks. Exhibit B would always be an old picture of me from when I was thin and showed no sign of a double chin (like when I was eleven). Then she'd remind me that the camera added about ten pounds, so I was actually even thinner than I looked in the pictures, which meant that I was in real trouble now, and it was a good thing she knew how to use the panorama button on her camera. Next up would be the fact that she herself has been the same weight for the last twenty-five years and was still wearing the exact same size tennis skirt from her twenties, and did I want to know the secret to her success. These days she didn't even bother waiting for me to nod my head yes, and she said that as soon as she went more than two pounds over her ideal weight, she immediately dropped carbs from her diet until it was gone.

Then I got to hear the part about how much she loves me, how she's only doing this for my own good as she knew it made me unhappy when I didn't look my best, and how I certainly didn't look my best when my face was fat. I always looked forward to this part, because it meant I was almost home free. Soon it would all be over because there are only two stages left to go, the humiliation stage (which is where she'd break me every time) and then finally the reward stage.

The humiliation stage involved her dragging out a scale that she had hidden somewhere close by. She'd demand that I get on it so we could figure out how much I needed to lose. As a result, I can no longer even look at a scale—whether at a gym or at a store—without my bottom lip starting to quiver in fear. In the last stage she would build me back up again. (I sometimes wonder whether she had been trained by the military at some point—maybe someone who specialized in interrogation—my mom could make a brick talk.) She would do this by telling me that she knew I could drop the weight easily and that as soon as I did she would buy me

Giving me her best dead-on stare, she said, "You're getting fat."

the expensive handbag I had been coveting (I'm in constant want of a new purse, and had once gained seven pounds on purpose just because I was dying for a Prada bag and I knew that once I lost the seven pounds she'd get it for me) or the new outfit that I had my eye on. I do well on the reward system.

I was a grown woman—now a grown married woman to boot, and my weight was really none of her business.

After I agreed with her, she just snapped her mouth closed and narrowed her eyes at me, trying to figure out whether my agreeing with her was some new defense strategy. She had been prepared for my normal theatrics where I'd start gesticulating wildly and stomp around the kitchen like a little girl throwing a temper tantrum while I told her that I was *not* a little girl and that she had better stop treating me like one. I would go on to say that I was a grown woman—now a grown married woman to boot, and my weight was really none of her business.

I said it again for emphasis, "Mom, you're right. I am getting fat."

Now she really didn't know what to do, as she had never built in a contingency for my actually agreeing with her right off the bat; it didn't seem as if she liked it very much either—perhaps it was too anticlimactic for her.

I bet that no good interrogator would want someone to spill her guts right away.

It was actually new territory for me as well, as my relationship with my mother has always been combative. The only times we were ever in agreement had to do with fashion and shopping, celebrities, or her assessment of the First Lady's new hairstyle. She is always right on the money when it comes to flattering hair, and she is masterful with accessories. On all other topics we clash like titans. She has always thought that I talk too loudly, laugh too much, and am too opinionated for a woman. I knew the thought of my ever landing a husband kept her up many nights during my twenties, as she was a member of the old school, really believing "a woman needed a man to take care of her." Her happiness knew no bounds when I told her that Cosmas and I were engaged; she was totally ecstatic. Every now and then I would try to talk to her about other things, like the time I told her that I was upset about having to leave all my friends and move to Boston for Cosmas's job. Her reply: "The man is the needle, the woman is the thread, wherever the needle goes, the thread shall follow." I mean, how does one even respond to such a thing?

Well, this time she was right—about my weight, that is. I told her that I had been in denial for months now, but recently I had finally accepted that I had fallen victim to the newlywed nineteen. The newlywed nineteen was the little-known cousin of the freshmen fifteen, which I had managed to avoid in college thanks to the fact that I spent the majority of my food money going out to dance clubs, the fact that I wore those tight little black Lycra dresses—the ones that showed no mercy—when I went out to dance clubs, and the fact that my mom sent me care packages that contained hand mirrors, scales, and salad dressing instead of cookies and chocolates.

I sort of crouched down a bit, only to realize that it was actually the sound of my mom shrieking.

Of course I had just made up the "newlywed nineteen." I was hoping my mom would be a little more understanding if she thought that this was a national phenomenon as opposed to just me and my new obsession with doughnuts. My favorites were coconut, then coconut chocolate, next would probably be a tie between strawberry frosted with sprinkles and the straight chocolate, and then . . .

I was broken out of my doughnut fantasy by a screeching noise that instinctively made me duck. There had to be a bird or bat in the house. I sort of crouched down a bit, only to realize that it was actually the sound

In Sickness and Health

of my mom shrieking "Nineteen? NINETEEN! NINE-
TEEN!!" over and over again in sheer disbelief. Hmmm,
she wasn't taking the news all too well, so I figured that
she probably didn't need to know that it was more like
twenty-two and three-eighths (a few years ago she had
bought me one of those atomic scales that are incredibly
exact and super-accurate and that measure one's weight
to the hundredth of a pound. I didn't use it for a really
long time because I was convinced that it must have some
kind of satellite communications mechanism that would
beam my weight back to my mother).

I had two defense strategies up my sleeve: First was the
old reversal-of-blame trick. I told her that I had just
been so happy lately (being married and all) that I just
hadn't even noticed that I had been putting on weight,
and I just hadn't realized it had gotten so out of control,
because she had always been my trusty watchdog about
such things. So then I asked her why she herself hadn't
noticed earlier and given me one of her usual pep talks
(that's what she likes to call them).

She told me that she hadn't seen me in the past five
months, and that whenever she asked me what I was
having for dinner when we talked on the phone, I would
always say "salad." Then she went for the big blow
and said that she'd also assumed that "you'd be watching

your figure a little more now that you have a husband to please."

My nostrils flared at this one, and I tried to remain calm, because she had basically walked right into my second defense strategy. "Actually, it's Cosmas's fault that I have gained so much weight, and did I happen to mention that he's put on a lot of weight, too, maybe even more than nineteen pounds?" I sat back in my chair with a satisfied look on my face, shouting in my head, "Nyah nyah nyah nyah nyaaaaaah!" (Sure, it's a known fact that no matter how old we get, we always seem to regress in the company of our parents, but sometimes it's really not so bad.)

Now the thing to know about my mom is that she looooooooves Cosmas. Cosmas could absolutely do no wrong in her eyes, and she always took his side even before she knew the story. She excused her behavior by saying some little phrase in Korean (I don't speak the language), which translated into something about a mother-in-law never having her shoes on when she runs out to meet her son-in-law because she's been SO BUSY CLEANING THE HOUSE AND MAKING ALL HIS FAVORITE FOODS FOR HIS ARRIVAL THAT BY THE TIME HE GETS THERE SHE DOESN'T EVEN HAVE TIME TO PUT ON HER SHOES! Can you even believe that one? You think I'm exaggerating? Well, I'm not. The first time we visited her for Christmas she had asked me in advance what his favorite drink was, and I told her that it was the lemon-lime Gatorade (which is sort of a hoot because Cosmas's idea of physical activity is having to make two trips to the trash), and right after she got us all set up in the living room (the room in which I'm never allowed to be), she came marching in the room carrying a silver tray with a bottle of Gatorade and a crystal highball glass full of ice. I still remember how I leapt to my feet and said, YOU HAVE GOT TO BE KIDDING ME, MOM, IT'S NOT LIKE HE'S ROYALTY, FOR PETE'S SAKE! I tried to tell her that she shouldn't spoil him like that, as I didn't want him to get too used to the good life, because the day I served him Gatorade in a glass that had to be hand washed, HA, that would be the day my shoes didn't match my handbag.

She asked me how it could possibly be sweet Cosmas's fault that I had gained nineteen pounds (twenty-three and five-eighths, but really, who's counting?). I told her that the first problem was that I never used to have food around when I lived alone and that now our fridge and pantry were full of food. The second problem was that Cosmas loved to snack late at night, and it's not as if I can let him sit on the couch all by himself eating chips and salsa, brownies, French-bread pizza, popcorn, and ice cream all by his lonesome, because we're a team, right? The third and last problem was that he's the first guy who I actually believed when he said that he'd love me no matter what, and he didn't care if I put on weight. He said he likes to see me happy, and if a doughnut will make me break out into song and dance, then let's buy a dozen.

She smiled at this and told me that I was lucky to have such an understanding husband. She told me that she understood how it happened and that she, too, had gained weight when she got married (not nineteen pounds, of course, but she had gained at least five, before instituting her golden two-pound rule). She then told me that if Cosmas liked me plump, then so be it; she wouldn't say another word about it.

That's it? No more lectures? No more threats? She shook her head no and told me that I was now a grown woman and if my husband was happy with my chubby cheeks then she was happy, too. This is when I got defensive and said that I was offended by the fact that as a woman it was my husband's point of view on my looks that mattered most. What about how I felt about my weight? What about my own opinion? I told her that even though Cosmas said he didn't mind that I had gained weight I minded; in fact, I minded a great deal. Besides, it's not as if I had to seek his approval all the time anyway. I told her I thought that not only did I need to lose the extra weight, but that he needed to as well. What about his newlywed nineteen? Why was all the pressure always put on the woman about such things? Why didn't he care how he looked for me? Then I announced there was no way I was going to stand for both of us letting ourselves go in such a shameful way. What about the next fifty years of pictures?

Enough was enough, we were both going to start a diet and begin to exercise more; I mean, we had to think of our health, right? My mom didn't say much either way, but she said that she'd be happy to buy us that new coffee table we were eyeing if we were both successful in our new mission. I then spent the next hour seeking her advice on the best way to bring up the topic with Cosmas. She gave me a few pointers and reminded me that men were just as sensitive about their weight as women were, so I needed to be careful not to hurt his feelings in any way.

Enough was enough, we were both going to start a diet and begin to exercise more.

Later that night, when Cosmas and I were sitting down to eat dinner (baked skinless chicken breast and a salad), I broached the subject as delicately as I could with him: "Cosmas, my mom thinks you're getting fat."

CHAPTER FIVE

For Better
or Worse

PING-PONG MARRIAGE STYLE

My older brother, John, and I had the typical big brother—little sister relationship while growing up. I would beg for rides to the mall for my friends and me, and he would make me clean his room while repeating that he was the king of the universe a hundred times over in exchange. In fact, when I was too young to know any better, my brother recruited me to be on his football team. This team consisted of him as the owner, coach, and starting quarterback, and me as the rest of the team (including waterboy). The first step was teaching me how to throw and catch a football—not like a girl, and not like a boy either, but like a Dallas Cowboy. And because it was the big leagues we didn't use one of those Nerf balls either—no, we played with the real regulation-size NFL leather ball—and at the end of each practice session I had the bruises to show for it. My entire chest and stomach were bright red as I learned that you don't catch the football with just your hands, you catch with your whole body—reaching for the ball and guiding it in to your stomach for a very secure catch.

I'm not sure how long we practiced, but it seemed like hours. It was at the end when we started running plays that he would outline with his fingers, using his chest as a chalkboard, how I should hut the ball to the quarterback and run up the field pretending to zigzag through the defense, either cutting a fast right or left and looking over my shoulder so I could catch the ball. Now, it was extremely important that I catch the ball, not just for the imaginary game of the imaginary team, but mainly because whenever I missed it I'd get in big trouble.

Sometimes, like when it was raining or when I was desperately tired and on the verge of keeling over, I wouldn't be able to catch the ball. The only person who was more upset than me for dropping the ball was, of course, my brother, who would morph from star Dallas Cowboys quarterback into Jimmy Johnson, the coach. In a flash he'd be in my face yelling at me, bellowing about what I did wrong, and finally at the end (the uplifting part) he'd scream at me, "NEVER COMPROMISE! NEVER COMPROMISE! NEVER COMPROMISE!" and he'd do this until I joined in so we were both screaming. Then he'd make me run three laps around the house as my punishment, and all the while I had to continue saying it. Never compromise. Never compromise. Never compromise.

Sure, 80 percent of our practice sessions ended with my running laps, my needing an icepack for a jammed thumb, or my being unable to watch my afternoon TV show because I had to sit and memorize my playbook, but there were days when I outran all the Steelers' defensemen (this was the '80s, so we only played against the Pittsburgh Steelers). When I caught every ball and executed each play flawlessly John would come over to me and pound me on the back, teach me how to spike the ball and do a little dance in the end zone; sometimes he'd even shake up a soda and spray it on me, like they do on TV with champagne. He really showed me that nothing was better than winning. Given all this, I'm pretty sure that if you surveyed a group of therapists, they would all agree that my brother could take some of the credit for the fact that I grew up to be incredibly demanding, hypercompetitive, and stubborn as a brick wall.

So now almost twenty years later, I would like to pass the buck to my brother regarding the fact that I wasn't so great at this notion of compromise, which made things a bit tricky after I got married. Compromise was one of those extremely popular marriage catchphrases that people doled out to you in the most casual way, like Tic Tacs. Trouble in paradise? Marriage is a compromise. Can't figure out who's right or wrong? Compromise. Angry that he's always late and never bothers to call and let you know? Tsk. Tsk. Compromise. (Not sure where the compromise lies in that one—perhaps not kill him but just maim him?) The gist was that marriage consisted of a great deal of tug-of-war, push and pull, give-and-take, back-and-forth, betwixt and between, which meant you had to learn how to meet in the middle, go along the middle of the road, find some middle ground, reach a happy medium, and pick and choose your battles. (How grand that you can boil down the most important relationship in your life into a simple catchy phrase.) But, to go with the flow, my favorite expression and the one that I have found to be the most accurate, was calling it all "Ping-Pong marriage style."

Compromise was one of those extremely popular marriage catchphrases that people doled out to you in the most casual way, like Tic Tacs.

After all, Ping-Pong is a pretty innocuous game (except when growing up in the Lee household—home of the ball-crushing overhead slams, and don't play if you're nervous about losing an eye) that was most enjoyable when there was a nice rally of back and forth. The great thing about Ping-Pong was that you could still win a lot of points even if you lost the game. It was actually a darling little girl who showed me the light on this one. The first time Cosmas and I played Ping-Pong together, while we were waiting for a table to open up at a pool hall (since I was saving my energy to pulverize him in our pool game, I was playing Ping-Pong in a very friendly and noncompetitive way), a ball got away from me. As I was trying to get the ball that had rolled under a video game, a little girl wandered over and retrieved it for me. She pointed over to Cosmas and asked whether he was my boyfriend. I said no, that we were married and he was my husband. Her next line will always stay with me because she said, "Married people play Ping-Pong so nice." I remember looking over at Cosmas and seeing him in a different light; it was true we were having a blast, and the game was much more fun when you tried to have a good rally over a quick win. I was feeling so enlightened at the time that I could have probably given up my desire to win the actual game right then and there if it hadn't been for the fact that when she asked me who was winning and I said that I was, she looked up at me and said, "You go, girl." But, the point was that when it comes to the millions of decisions you have to deal with in marriage—big and small—it was a good idea to handle them the way you play Ping-Pong—playing for fun over playing for blood, er, I mean, playing to win.

WHEN I WAS ON THE PHONE WITH MY FRIEND JACKIE, bemoaning the fact that Cosmas and I had to find a new apartment and move, she was nice enough to let me know that moving was third on the list of life's most stressful experiences *ever,* right after death and divorce. I then tried to make a joke of it by saying that perhaps "moving" got shortchanged, because if it's really that bad, it could potentially cause the first two. I gave a hearty chuckle and waited for Jackie to join in. Jackie didn't laugh. That should have been my first sign.

Right after we married we moved to Boston, but I don't consider that our first real marriage move. Mainly because it was more of a "me-moving" experience versus a "we-moving" experience—I found the apartment by myself, I moved from New York City first, and then he moved (after I packed his stuff) from New Haven a few months later. So I'm really the one who got settled in first, papered the shelves, figured out where everything went, picked out which closet would be mine, etc. And, because we were both so swamped with work, we never really settled in. Ten months later we hadn't even finished unpacking all our boxes, and we never even put one picture up on the wall. Sometimes we'd talk about it over takeout. He'd say, "Y'know, we should really put up a few pictures." Then I'd say, "Yeah, we should. Why don't you put some up this weekend?" But he never did, and I didn't mind, because we had waited too long. We had lost the move-in momentum, when finding and putting up pictures would have been a new adventure as opposed to just another item on our never-ending to-do lists.

So after we found out we had to move again, we made a pact and decided that this time we'd make it different. This time it would be a joint effort and we'd make it fun. We would find a great place together, pack up our stuff together, move in together, unpack together, and decorate together. (At this point someone should have checked us both into a sanitarium together.) At the very least we swore to actually get a utensil tray as opposed to having all our silverware jumbled up in a drawer the way we had for the past year.

The first thing to note about doing things together is that it takes much more time than doing things on your own. The two-heads-are-better-than-one rule does not apply to apartment hunting. Mainly because you went from noting the pros and cons of each apartment to having to discuss each one at great length. So we'd see an apartment that had a tiny kitchen with no counter space, and I'd say, "The kitchen is way too small. There's not enough counter space." I thought I was just making a declarative statement, but I soon discovered that wasn't at all what I was doing. Actually I was offering up a problem, and Cosmas was a classic male in the sense that he felt that every problem had a solution. This trait was extremely useful when you're a doctor, but it can be a bit annoying at times that didn't qualify as life-and-death situations.

The two-heads-are-better-than-one rule does not apply to apartment hunting.

So he would thoughtfully scratch his chin and say something like, "Well, we could always get one of those carts on wheels that would give you more counter space." So then we'd do a little back and forth in terms of where we would put such a cart, where we would buy such a cart, why he said "you" vs. "us" and why I found that to be a really chauvinistic comment, how much such a cart would cost, whether we could find one with a chopping board built in, dark wood over light. . . . Eventually we made our way to wondering whether the hassle of finding and buying such a cart would even be worth it. It wouldn't.

Keep in mind that this was just one consideration about any given apartment and when you factor in number of bedrooms, layout, bathroom, size, sunlight, walk up, neighborhood, and parking, the real estate agent would give us a wild-eyed look, where it was fifty-fifty in terms of whether he wanted to kill us or himself. Heck, after seeing a few more places I met his gaze and gave him an eyebrow signal letting him know that he should just kill us. At the end of the day he politely suggested we'd cover more ground if we split up and did first looks alone and then saw the places that made the cut together. He said we'd save time, and, oh by the way, he forgot to mention that he was actually leaving the next day for an extended trip abroad so we would need to find another realtor to help us.

So then we hashed out the top three attributes we each wanted from an apartment: mine were lots of space, proximity to a decent deli, and good closets. Cosmas's were availability of parking, trash drop-off location (he hated our last apartment because he had to carry the trash bags half a block to the corner of the street, and pick up was only on designated days), and the price. Inevitably the apartments that made it to final round always had the attributes that one of us wanted, but rarely had the ones that the other wanted. It was another exasperated real estate person who advised us to sit down together and figure out the top three attributes combined. Hours of tense negotiations later, we were back on the streets searching for an apartment that had lots of space with large closets, a decent deli nearby, and either lots of parking inventory or a trash drop-off that was fewer than twenty-five steps from the front door.

Eventually the gods must have taken pity on us (or on the real estate agents) and we had one of those experiences where we got a call to come see a place when we happened to be together, we looked at each other and promised to be on our best behavior, and we went. Both of us walked in with absolutely no expectations at all, and the best part about having no expectations is that every positive trait was suddenly a big bonus. It's got windows! Running water! A closet! We were both quiet as we surveyed the whole place; only when we walked back into the hall at the end did we meet each other's gaze, and together we said, "We'll take it," since it also had most of the other attributes we had been looking for as well. The real estate agent smiled and said it was nice to work with a couple so in sync with each other, because most other young married couples were pretty annoying. Cosmas and I nodded our agreement because we had both heard similar things, too.

WHEN IT COMES TO MOVING into a new apartment with someone, especially someone who isn't a temporary room-mate, but a lifelong one—you have to prepare yourself for debates about a lot of random things you never thought you cared about. It started small, like the fact that Cosmas always put glasses upside down in the cabinets and I put them right-side up. He felt that his way protected the inside of the glass from dust particles landing in the glass, but I begged to differ, pointing out that by having the glasses upside down they would get dirty around the all-important rim, which received full mouth contact. All you needed was a smidgen of bacteria and then *bam*, those babies would start to multiply like rabbits in the petri dishes that are our mouths. So what if a little dust got into the bottom of the glass, whatever beverage you drank would just wash it down to your stomach where it would quickly be neutralized by your stomach acid. My gastroenterologist husband rolled his eyes at my pseudoscientific blather, and I tickled him until he admitted that my logic was more or less sound. But he still liked his way better. Needless to say the glasses were right-side up 90 percent of the time since I was the one who always happened to empty the dishwasher, so there hadn't been much reason even to discuss it.

Next was divvying up the scarce bathroom shelving provided. The bathroom had a teeny tiny mirrored medicine chest with sliding doors and two shelves. I told Cosmas that I was going to take the shelves and offered him the back of the toilet for his stuff. This, of course, turned into a discussion about who spent more time in the bath-room, which, oddly enough, was him (long showers, lots of time fussing about in front of the mirror), who had more products (me, but that was more because I was a compulsive drugstore shopper), who actually used more products (that was a toss-up because if makeup was counted then it was def-initely me, if not it was a tie due to all of his shaving paraphernalia), and whose time was actually used for pur-chasing said products (this was my suggestion, because I needed to even the score). His final contribution was that since I was shorter than him (by like four inches) I should get the back of the toilet because it was closer to the ground. Oh, please. What it came down to was that we didn't have enough space in the bathroom. Suddenly I had an idea—the best way to resolve the issue was to buy and put up one of those bathroom shelf units with doors. I could put all my stuff in the new cabinet, and he could have the shelves in the medicine chest. Easy enough. This was when he gallantly agreed to take the back of the toilet, but by then it was too late, I had already written "buy and put up bathroom cabi-net" on his to-do list that was clipped to the fridge. This was actually a great lesson in choosing your battles wisely.

For certain things there was no debate at all. I got the bigger closet; I got more dresser drawers; I got the nicer bedside table (but that was only because my side of the bed was always the one closest to the door, so my bedside table was more visible). He got to position the TV and couch however he wanted; he got to decide where the wall hangings went (I had one veto vote). Actually, that was all he got free reign to decide.

The biggest controversy was over two things that weren't even in the apartment: the buzzer and the mailbox. A few days after we had moved in, I was surprised to see that someone had put our name on the labels for the buzzer and the mailbox. I assumed it was the landlord, but when I studied the stickers a bit more closely, I recognized Cosmas's penmanship. He had incredibly neat handwriting for a guy and especially for a doctor, and he had meticulously spelled out in all *caps* G-I-A-L-L-O-U-R-A-K-I-S, and that was it. I sighed when I saw it, because I either had to leave it be, or we were once again going to play Ping-Pong on the topic of my changing my name.

A woman changing her name in New York City was a hot topic and was usually the third question I was asked when someone found out that I was engaged (the first two were when's the wedding, and how did he propose). My response was normally a shrug, followed by my saying that

I guess I would, but that when it came to my professional life I'd always use my maiden name. It was a pretty quick and pat answer that sounded quite reasonable at the time.

I guess I had never really given the matter much thought due to the spell of the sparkly and my inability to see life after the dress. So I had just gone with the flow, which was that Cosmas, my mom, and my in-laws all assumed I'd change my name. All through the honeymoon I was called Mrs. Giallourakis, and I got used to having to spell and pronounce it for anyone who came across it. It was on the plane heading back to the States when Cosmas said that his father could help me with the

I never got around to changing my name, and the longer I put it off, the more I realized that I didn't really want to change it.

paperwork involved when I changed my name. I gave him a quizzical look, and he said, not asked, "You are changing your name, right." His voice made me a bit tense, so I said that I guessed so, but what's with all the paperwork. He explained that it was a legal process that involved filing papers and signing official documents. But what he didn't say was that it also involved making hundreds of phone calls and wasting my life away listening to soft rock while on hold as I switched over everything from my social security card to all my department-store credit cards. The whole thing sounded like a huge headache, but I said I'd look into it when we got back just so I could go back to reading my fashion magazine (when we stopped off in Barbados, I had shelled out big bucks to get the latest fashion mags after having spent the last ten days without them).

I never got around to changing my name, and the longer I put it off, the more I realized that I didn't really want to change it. My name had been so good to me for so many years—short and sweet, and apparently there was an old song from the '30s about a Jenny Lee from Tennessee. On more than one occasion I had had a sixty-plus man sing it to me over the phone. As far as I knew, there were no songs about a Jenny Giallourakis. Now I wouldn't go so far as to say I was duplicitous in any way, or that I even pretended to have legally changed my name, but a jury of my peers could probably convict me on intent to be sneaky. Slowly I started accruing membership cards with my married name on them, so the grocery store, the pharmacist, and the movie rental people all knew me as Jenny Giallourakis. Whenever Cosmas was within earshot, I'd make all reservations under the Giallourakis name, but when he wasn't around I put them under Lee.

One day he busted me because I accidentally intro-duced myself as Jenny Lee to someone at one of his work functions. I caught my gaffe immediately, but it was too late, because the person said, "Oh, you didn't take his name?" (Can't people mind their own business?) And I felt my face grow hot and my response ran along the line of "Abooidfhglkehs sdhf," which was partially due to Cosmas's boa-constrictor grip on my right hand. Cosmas just smiled through gritted teeth, pulled me aside, and asked me point-blank about it. While trying to shake a little bit of blood back into my fingers, I told him the truth—that I had lost the change of name packet that I had ordered and I needed to call and get another one. Okay, I lied. But I just wasn't prepared to have such a big conversation at the time, and besides, it certainly would have gotten in the way of our let's-see-who-can-eat-the-most-free-jumbo-cocktail-shrimp contest.

Did it really matter anyway? I would certainly answer to Giallourakis, and I wouldn't do the feminist flip-out if anyone called me that or sent me letters addressed that way. I'd even yuck it up with the people who thought it was a hoot to say, "Well, you certainly don't look Greek." I wanted to tell everyone that they should lighten up about the whole matter, I mean, legal shmegal—didn't I change my primary e-mail address to jgiallourakis? In the age of the Internet, that was as committed as you could get.

I'm not sure why but Cosmas never brought it up again, and neither did I. But now what should I do about the mailbox and buzzer? The majority of my mail still had my maiden name, and if anyone who had met me as Jenny Lee was ever looking for me, then they'd have no idea to look for me under Giallourakis. Being a total chicken, I decided to let sleeping dogs lie; in very small lettering right underneath Cosmas's fine handwriting, I wrote "Lee" in parentheses.

Cosmas, who never noticed anything, who could never find his keys even though they were right there on the table by the door, who needed help finding his glasses most mornings, saw my addendum the very first time he went outside. Lucky for me I wasn't with him at the time, so I didn't have to witness his facial expression or the smoke and fire that probably shot out of his nose.

I heard him before I saw him, which was probably because he was barreling up the stairs yelling my name. When he threw open the door to face me, I was armed and ready with a copy of Strunk and White that I waved around to distract him. I quickly told him that by having "Lee" in parentheses, it was actually not a stand-alone name but was really a parenthetical of Giallourakis, making it virtually one and the same, and that it wasn't like I put a slash mark and then "Lee," which would have definitely shown a complete separation. I could tell that he wasn't going for this line of reasoning, and I tried to think of an appropriate analogy to give him—something mathematical like $(a + b) = (a + c)$, as long as $(b = c)$, but I didn't have any chalk—so I took a deep breath and said, "I've decided that I don't want to change my name."

Silence.

More silence.

Heavy breathing on his part.

No breathing on my part.

In a sad voice he said, "So your Blockbuster card was just a lie?" Those eight words nearly broke my heart, and if someone had handed me a name-change form right then and there, I would have caved, but instead I tried my best to explain to him that of course I was a Giallourakis because I was his wife and we were definitely a team— Team Giallourakis to be exact, but couldn't I still be Jenny Lee as well?

More silence.

I continued, telling him there was no question of our future children and puppies being Giallourakises, not a hyphen in sight. I told him that in all nonbusiness correspondence I would always sign my name as Jenny Giallourakis, so every holiday card from now until forever would state "Season's Greetings from the Giallourakis Family."

More silence but no more heavy breathing.

Tentatively I went up to him, put my arms around his waist, burrowed my face into his chest, and begged him not to be mad at me.

Eventually I felt him relax. He told me he wasn't mad but he wasn't happy either. He asked me if my mind was completely made up, no chance of my ever changing it? I told him that it was made up for now, but who knows what would happen in the future, because marriage was about compromise. And there could be a day when I might need it as a bargaining chip.

O, CHRISTMAS TREE, O, SANDRA DEE . . .

In addition to playing Scrabble and Ping-Pong, now that I am married I frequently have to play a variation of keeping-up-with-the-Joneses that I call the Great American Couple-off (GACO for short). It's easy to do because all it takes is seeing some young couple massively making out on a street corner, and I have to think, When was the last time we made out like that in public? Which leads to, Did we ever make out like that? (Yes, but it had been a while.) Or when I see a couple packing up the car with their ski equipment, off for a weekend of hitting the slopes, and even though I don't ski I wonder whether they are a better couple because they do. Yes, the Great American Couple-off is a slippery slope, but what I try to remember is that every couple is different, and different does not mean better.

My favorite form of procrastination is to go down my phone speed-dial list of friends and call everyone I know. My best friend Laura is, of course, number one. For the record, Laura, bless her soul, does not give good phone, so our phone conversations are usually brief and very efficient—meaning we tend to drill down a list of items that we might not be caught up with. Work? Check. Family? Check. New clothing purchases? Check. Always leaving the best for last . . . the darling men in our lives.

I usually get the ball rolling, "AND, how's the fiancé?"

Laura was the perfect case of a woman who was now completely under the spell of the sparkly. She had it bad. When she called to tell me that Chris proposed, I was able to figure out her news based on her first three spoken syllables. I answered the phone saying hello my normal way. There was a split-second pause, and then I heard her say, "Hey, it's me," but this was no ordinary "Hey-it's-me"-I'm-bored-at-work-and-just-calling-to-say-hello-and-see-what's-new-with-you, no, this was the happiest "Hey, it's me" I had ever heard from her, and we've been best friends for ten years plus, so it's not as if I haven't heard her ecstatic. Up to this point, her happiest "Hey, it's me's" have always been just after she got her hair done; Laura's got a thing about great hair. This "Hey, it's me" was different; this was the "Hey, it's me" of marching bands playing, a thousand angels singing, and those seven swans from that Christmas song singing away. Instantly I

My favorite form of procrastination is to go down my phone speed-dial list of friends and call everyone I know.

shrieked, "Ohmygod, he didn't!" and she screamed, "He did!" and I said, "When?" and she said, "Last night on the roof with six dozen roses!" and I shouted, "Tell me more, tell me more, what were you wearing?" She said she happened to be wearing pajamas but her hair was to die for, and then we both almost started crying.

Now, it's almost seven months later, but whenever I call her and ask about her future husband she's all moony and drunk on love. "Heeeee's wooooonnnnnderful."

I roll my eyes, not being bitchy, because, of course, I was happy that she was happy, and I was happy that he was so damn wonderful. *But* what I wasn't happy about was that when she's all Look-at-me, I'm-Sandra-Dee, that leaves me no choice but to fall into the role of the sarcastic Rizzo, and Rizzo would roll her eyes.

She squealed, "Oh, oh—guess what?!"

I didn't respond. Rizzo doesn't play guessing games.

Sandy kept going. "Chris and I got our very first Christmas tree on Saturday!"

This sparked some interest from me, because Cosmas and I actually got our first Christmas tree on Saturday, too. So I got to be Sandy for a second, "Reaalllly, hooowww funnnnny, we did, too."

But she started the story, so the rules say she gets to go first. She continued gushing, "I'm now officially in the Christmas spirit. It was so great. I mulled some hot apple cider while he was getting it set up in the tree stand. So then we put on the stand cover, which I got from Gumma (her late grandmother). It's just beautiful; she made it by hand for her very first tree. Can you imagine?"

I couldn't.

"Then we had a little tree-decorating party, just the two of us. We put on all the lights first, and then all the ornaments—"

I broke in, "What about tinsel? I love tinsel."

"I like tinsel, too, but it's a little messy . . ." She doesn't miss a beat. "Sooooo, then we realized that we only have about two dozen ornaments, and did you know that ornaments, well, the nice ones, are really expensive? So Chris and I made a pact that every Christmas from now on we'd buy each other one beautiful ornament as a stocking stuffer, so by the time we were old we would have this amazing collection. The best part is that every single one of them will have deep sentimental value because we picked them out for each other. Your turn."

I now realized that I'm actually on the phone and not in a Hallmark commercial gone somehow horribly awry. "Oh, well, there's really not much to tell. We found this tree at a flower shop on the corner, and I tracked down a tree stand. It took Cosmas about thirty minutes to figure out how to assemble the tree stand, and then another thirty minutes to get the tree upright."

I heard that my voice was losing its luster, so I sat up on the couch and tried to give it a grand finale. "I just looooove having a tree; it makes the apartment smell really great."

She's obviously pleased that I have started to try a little, so she chimed in, "Ooooh, yeah, yeah, ours too. What kind did you get, Norway Spruce or Dutch Fir? I loved the way the fir looked, but the needles start to fall off and it would get a little . . ."

I wrinkled my nose and mouthed the word silently along with her, "messy."

I actually scratched my head at this question. "You know, I have no idea what kind of tree it is. I don't think it's the kind with the messy needles though. It really is nice and it sure does smell great."

She's in total I'm-a-little-teapot mode, and her words are pouring out. "Soooooooo?" she asked, her voice rising up in festive anticipation.

"So what?" I asked back. I imagined her wearing a pink organza dress with white-gloved hands clasped together in front of her in childlike glee. Pink handbag and a pair of darling pink strappy sandals. I mean, Sandy certainly had style, I'll give her that. "What about the decorations?"

I thought about lying here, but I didn't. "Well, I haven't really had a chance to get any ornaments yet, but Cosmas's mom sent one to us in the mail. It's cute. It's a little red Santa Claus. I put it front and center. It's really nice." I fought the urge to bring up the great tree smell again.

Sandy was silent.

I sucked it up and continued, "But we did buy some white lights. Though we haven't had a chance to put them on yet. Y'know Cosmas—he was a little tired from getting the tree up the two flights of stairs, and the battle with the tree stand just finished him off. He promised to put them on later, and of course I'll help. We'll put them on together."

I started sounding fake, so I quickly switched subjects. A tricky little dance move, but I think I pulled it off, "So, did you guys go the star route or the reindeer route?"

"Actually, we couldn't decide, because at my house we always had an angel growing up, but Chris's family always had a star. So I found this beautiful crystal ornament that's an angel sitting on top of star!" I know that even she perceived that this was a little precious, so she plowed on through. "But I was so scared Chris would knock the whole damn tree over while he was on top of the chair. You know how he's not the most coordinated guy." That's a gimmie on her part; she was just being nice because we both know that Chris had never taken a false step in his life. Whereas Cosmas . . .

Before I can stop myself, it flew out of my mouth, "Chair?" (Chris is over six feet tall.)

"We went for an eight-and-a-half-footer. Barely got it through the door!"

What was I thinking? I mean, c'mon—I was already lying flat out on my back on the mat, and the match was basically over. But no, I just had to get back up. I was just standing there begging for the final knockout—the fatal right hook. Best friend or not, she had to do it; I wouldn't respect her if she didn't.

"Why? How tall is your tree?"

LIE! JUST LIE! FOR GOD'S SAKE, IT'S BEEN A MASSACRE. JUST SAY IT'S THE BIGGEST TREE YOU'VE EVER SEEN. TELL HER PAUL BUNYAN'S WIFE WOULD BE PROUD. YOU'VE ALREADY LOST, DIE WITH A LITTLE DIGNITY.

But I just don't have the heart to lie. "Well, I'd say it's a good four and three-quarters feet." (It's maybe four feet at best, but though I didn't have the heart to lie, I sure had the stomach to stretch the truth. Hell, it's human nature to round up—except perhaps when it comes to your weight.)

Let me break in for moment and say Laura's next comment was totally sincere and truly genuine, even though it was the winning blow. Brace yourself, this one's gonna hurt.

"Well, it must be very cute; everything is cute when it's small."

Suddenly I must be just about the cutest woman alive, because I'm feeling maybe six inches tall (rounding up), a Rizzo Barbie wearing a badass leather jacket . . .

Shortly thereafter, our call came to an end. I got off the phone and peeled myself off the mat. I walked over to our short stubby tree, with its one scarlet ornament of shame dangling on it . . . and I winced, waiting for all those dark wretched thoughts to start bubbling to the surface.

Stupid-short-patchy-assed-one-ornament-bearing tree.

Yeah, no one's going to be singing songs about your sorry ass.

Tree? You're no tree, you'd be lucky to pass for an overdeveloped shrub.

But it didn't happen. In fact, none of those thoughts came up at all. Instead I looked at our very first married-person tree with something like pride. Cosmas and I were busy little campers, and I was proud that we had even managed to get one at all. I was thrilled that Cosmas was able to put the stand together all by himself, without my help or my having to call my older brother. We had fun putting it up. We held hands and admired it. And he kissed me in front of it, making some reference to mistletoe that didn't quite make sense, but that I somehow totally understood, and I loved him all the more for it. In fact, I'm tickled pink with our one and only ornament. Lights? Lights are overrated.

I will admit that it was missing one thing though, but I swore to race out and get it, right then and there.

TINSEL. Rizzo would approve.

THE PERFECT FIGHT

As many cute and funny stories that anyone has about her marriage, there are always a few stories that no one talks about. My mother and Mary Sunshine are in perfect agreement over the fact that it's not polite to air one's dirty laundry in public and that *certain* things are nobody's business, but I feel that I must be fair to all the new wives out there and let them in on the fact that married people, even extremely happily married people, do fight from time to time. Now this is a given, but I'm going to go one step further and let everyone in on the fact that sometimes happily married people can have a big huge massive horrendous fight—one that really is not quite appropriate to discuss at a dinner party unless you want everyone to lean away from you (fear of its being contagious)—and that they *can* get through it. I call this type of fight "a perfect fight" (as in "the perfect storm") mainly because they are rare (thank goodness) and come about only when the stars align just so.

Perfect fights have similarities to all natural disasters, the subtle buildup, the quick eruption, the destructive power, and the damage left behind. After a tornado destroys the barn, you build another one, a better one. After a hurricane destroys a village, you build another village in its place, with a larger ice-cream parlor. After locusts destroy this season's crops, you patiently sow more seeds and wait till next spring.

When I was small and scared of thunderstorms, my father would come in and explain to me how it worked, what was inside those dark clouds, what made the lightning and the noise. I was still afraid but less so because he taught me how to fight my fear with knowledge. So let's look inside a perfect fight and deconstruct it; let's see what makes it start and how you'll know when it's over. There are no preventative measures that you can take against having one in your own marriage, but maybe if you understand how they work you'll be less afraid if you ever get caught in one. At the insistence of my mom (What would the Bible study group think?) and Mary Sunshine (Do you really need the neighborhood wives goin' after your husband like flies to a dead pig? Gee, I guess not.)

Sometimes happily married people can have a big huge massive horrendous fight.

I'm going to omit the "specific dirty laundry details" of our particular perfect fight and just break it down for you in a blueprint fashion so you can see how one works.

One reason why perfect fights are so rare is because there must be a slow and simultaneous buildup that occurs on both sides. Perhaps one person had to make a sacrifice that was turning out to be too big, something that was taking too much out of her. She tries to remain stoic, but there are days when she feels a twinge of resentment. (Take, for example, a woman who is getting married and being forced to move five hundred miles from her favorite place in the world—Bergdorf Goodman—and then whose husband works all the time so she doesn't have any friends with whom to watch the Thursday night NBC lineup.) At the same time her spouse was well aware of the sacrifice and couldn't stand the stony stoicism she was showing and he was beginning to resent feeling guilty over it. (Cosmas noted that Bergdorf's is owned by Nieman Marcus, a branch of which is conveniently located in the city of Boston. This was an obvious sign of his guilt as he would never normally encourage shopping.) Another component of the buildup is simply a small ongoing battle between husband and wife. Something small and trivial but after many small battles there are wounds that never get a proper chance to heal. (Like those pesky mosquito bites that you can't help but scratch.)

Of course, communication can certainly alleviate this buildup, but, as open as a husband and wife can be, both always have a few thoughts that they never share because they are petty, selfish, and they feel shame for even thinking such things.

Next is the second phase of buildup: it's what was called the extraneous short-term buildup. This usually takes place from one to four days before the actual fight breaks out. Again, this buildup must occur on both sides, but it usually has little to do with the other person. These were just dumb luck, in the sense that both of you happened to have one or even a string of a few bad days in a row resulting from little annoyances that we face in the outside world. Cosmas and I consider ourselves lucky because for the first eight or nine months of our marriage, when one of us had a bad day, the other hadn't, so we were able to take turns being the cheerleader and the sympathizer. The first time we both had a bad day simultaneously (previous to our perfect fight) we were somehow smart enough to realize it and avoided each other for the rest of the evening. We were not so smart the second time.

Now, the bad days I'm talking about aren't those one-or-two-annoying-things-happened-so-I'm-a-bit-pissy-and-agitated days. No, the extraneous short term buildup required those really awful, wretched days that consist of a minimum of five, if not eight, of the following, in combination, per day: slight headache, runny noise, itchy eye, slight lingering cold, lost item, something spilled, something broken or torn or run, rudeness of a stranger, boss yelling at you, ridiculed by some snot-nosed teenager, bad hair day, two bad hair days in a row, a parking ticket, a traffic jam, a fender bender that wasn't your fault, a fender bender that was your fault, cable acting up, TV on the blink, someone bought the last one in your size three minutes earlier, experiment didn't work, experiment didn't work the second time, ATM out of service, no stamps, alarm didn't go off, alarm went off but you set it for the wrong time, service charge on a credit card bill for a payment that was one day late, fight with your mother, long line, forgotten keys or wallet or lipstick, burned bagel, two-pound weight gain, a six-pound weight gain (any weight gain over five pounds counts as two items), sat on hold via speakerphone for twenty minutes or longer and then pushed the wrong button when the operator picked up and the phone disconnected, lost your favorite pen, forgot to call a friend on her birthday, didn't get the job, didn't get the promotion, worst enemy got the promotion, forgot your cell phone or briefcase or scarf in a cab, crowded subway, broken crowded subway, burned your tongue so you had those little blisters that last a surprisingly long time, paper cut, Xerox machine jammed again, hair in your sandwich, broken nail, smudged manicure, shaving cut, big pimple, no more oatmeal chocolate chip at the cafeteria by the time you make it down for lunch, bowl of cereal and milk gone bad, rain, rain and suede shoes, rain and suede shoes with no umbrella standing on the corner and a car splashed you, lost dry cleaning, forgot to drop off dry cleaning, why is it that I'm always the one who has to deal with the dry cleaning?, out of milk, out of orange juice, out of microwave popcorn, out of Advil, out of patience, and finally, out of your mind.

So now you have had a stretch of four of these awful wretched days (any more than four and you should call in sick to work and stay in bed the next day because it's reported that five can be fatal to you or others), you are frazzled, you are tired, you are way beyond tense, you are now capable of making faces and performing actions that could make little kids cry and telemarketers hang up on *you* for a change. *And* to top it all off, your spouse has had an equally really awful, wretched day.

Now comes the trigger moment, the thing that causes the perfect storm to erupt. I have heard from others that the trigger moment is always a small, trite, not-a-big-deal thing, but given the background of the slow internal buildup and the extraneous short-term buildup, it's understandable how the wrong look or word or action could be the match that ignites the whole thing. Our trigger moment was completely absurd and involved the wrong drink. I had just gotten home and was sitting on the couch fuming over my really awful, wretched day.

Cosmas came in a few minutes later from an equally really awful, wretched day. He said, "I stopped at the deli and bought drinks." No hello. No kiss. He opened his own Diet Coke and handed me the bag. Inside the bag was a Sunkist orange soda. I have nothing against orange soda, and I can see why it's popular for its fizz and its tangy taste, but it just so happened that I personally do not care for orange soda. In fact, I probably hadn't had an orange soda in maybe twenty years. So I'm just staring at it, and the only words that came out of my mouth were "Orange soda?" So he said, "What's wrong with orange soda?," meaning I should feel lucky that he got me anything at all. And I said, "Have you ever seen me drink an orange soda?" in a tone that meant "proceed with extreme caution." He said, "I don't know, probably not," meaning I dare you to keep going. So I said, "Then what on earth would possess you to buy me a Sunkist orange soda when you should know that the only soda I drink is Diet Coke." Meaning I was about to lose it. He said, "I dunno," meaning today of all days I will not deal with your crap. So I'm wondering how I managed to marry the most oblivious, unobservant man in the world. Did he not care to know my drink of choice when I can name every drink he likes and put them in the order of his preference depending on his mood, what he's eating, and where we are.

And so began the perfect fight. Perfect fights do not build up to loud; perfect fights start out loud and build up to incredibly loud. The energy that fills the room is electric, and both people act as if they are possessed. The fight quickly moves from the trigger issue to whatever big issue has just passed or is on the horizon, combined with anything else about which they are currently annoyed at the other. There are no rules in a perfect fight, and there is no regard whatsoever for feelings. Before they can even make it through one topic a new one is introduced, fuel for the fire. Every single dumb annoying thing that the spouse has done in the past few months is suddenly fair game and shoved in each other's face. The time when I said I had to pee when we were on our way home from dinner and when we walked in the door he went into the bathroom and peed first. The time I asked him to stop by the store to pick up some Windex and then found an extra bottle in the closet. I don't mean to minimize the severity of a per-

Perfect fights do not build up to loud; perfect fights start out loud and build up to incredibly loud.

fect fight, because it truly is a miserable experience. It's just that the reason it causes so much damage and goes on for so long is because your normal ability to keep yourself in check is not working, you have bulldozed the fence and there are no boundaries. Both parties cross the line in so many different ways. Both hurt the other's feelings on purpose. Both say things they regret. Both say things that aren't even true. Both scream until they are hoarse; both cry; both break something or throw something; both say that they hate the other; both call the other names; both say they will never forgive the other.

The fight goes on for hours, and you are lucky that the cops don't show up, but maybe it would have been better if they did. By the end you are both red-faced, bleary-eyed, and sitting on the floor, hunched over from all the damage that has been inflicted. You feel as if you have just been to war (you have), and you both feel a tightness in the chest from hearts that were not just broken but pulled apart with bare hands and chewed up raw and thrown up and spit into the gutter of despair. (You think I'm being overly dramatic, but, sadly, I am not.) Later you will not remember how it even ended, but thank God it did.

This eerie silence is the time in a normal fight when you both sort of look at each other and either start to laugh or to apologize, but not this time. This time too much has been said. This time you have both gone too far. This time you still feel hatred in your heart but have fallen silent, resulting from exhaustion and lack of saliva; you even consider licking off some of the drops of orange soda on your arm. (At one point I shook it up and actually tried to spray him with it, but he grabbed my hands and tried to get the can away so we were both covered; I was finding sticky orange soda drops months later.) But you don't speak, which is a good thing because you wouldn't say anything nice anyway. This time you are scared because you are wondering whether your marriage is now over. (It isn't.) This time you are sad because right now, right here in this very moment, one of the worst moments of your entire

But you don't speak, which is a good thing because you wouldn't say anything nice anyway.

life, you don't even know if you care if it's over. (You do, but that's how you feel.) Then you start to cry.

So you're thinking, Now what? What next? How does a couple survive such a tragedy? I cannot speak for others, but we did not speak to each other for days. We did not touch; we did not acknowledge each other's existence. There was an incredible fatigue that ruled my world, and everything was fuzzy and tears ran down my face at odd times. It was Cosmas who finally spoke the first words. "Pack a bag; we're going to Vermont for the weekend." I said I'd rather go to hell. Unfortunately, there was a lot of collateral damage in the aftermath, and it was gravity that pulled these petty comments out of me and threw them to the ground. But I packed my bag anyway and told him I hated Vermont. He told me he hated my attitude. These pissing matches don't ever build because all your reserves are spent, so they taper off into silence after a few refrains.

The car ride was silent and pretty uneventful, except for when he bought me another orange soda as a joke and I started to cry. We were staying in a ski town, and I was surprised to see it bustling. Cosmas informed me that we were very lucky even to get a room because the entire town was totally booked up for leaf-peeping season. "Wow, they've got some racket going here. This has nothing to do with nature at all, this stupid leaf-peeping season is just a big sham to get all these inns and restaurants full before ski season starts." He called me a sourpuss, and I said, "So what if I am?"

So this was the part where I am supposed to say that everything was soon all better, and that we had the best time of our lives. That I was now the newest disciple in the cult of the great outdoors. Well, sorry to disappoint, but that wasn't what happened. What really happened was that we had a fight on our first night there, or rather, I managed to get us into a fight on our first night. We did manage a few scattered moments of niceness or shared laughter (it was truly hard to be mean when eating ice cream), but they were far outnumbered by bad moments. By Sunday morning I was pretty sure Cosmas deeply regretted trying to make amends at all. He used going out to get the Sunday *Times* as an excuse to get away for a while. (Perhaps with hopes that my unpleasantness was all a result of withdrawal symptoms from not having read the Sunday Styles section before ten A.M.) After he left I wondered whether he'd even come back at all. Wasn't that the way it worked in the movies, the husband going off in search of cigarettes or a loaf of bread, never to be seen again? Which would leave me, well, husbandless I guess. This thought made me a little sad, because even though he was driving me crazy as of late, I certainly didn't want to live my life without him. This gave me a brief spark of hope that all was not lost. Yes, the more I thought about it, the more I was completely sure that I wanted him to come back. Finally, a good sign.

He returned an hour later empty-handed. "C'mon, crankpot (my new nickname), I checked us out. Let's go."

Hooray, we were leaving. I was almost thankful finally to go back to Boston, which was a first. I kept myself in check and didn't say that out loud. We packed in silence, and I was feeling a little bad because I was probably more responsible for ruining the weekend than he was. It was obvious by his stiffness that he, too, wasn't quite over the perfect fight, but he was at least trying to make things better. When we got in the car, I decided to apologize for my behavior over the past two days (no way I was apologizing for the big fight), but before I could say anything, he announced that he had booked us on a two-hour horseback-riding tour through the mountains. I was stunned. This was a very un-Cosmas thing to do; he was not really the proactive type, and he was rarely the creative one. Desperate times. Desperate measures.

Soon I was astride a big brown mare named Shalimar (I'm totally serious), following behind Cosmas, who was riding Lucky Buck, and our husky country cowboy tour guide, Chuck, who was riding Pretty Lady (how unoriginal). It was much colder in the mountains, but the air smelled great. I was in complete awe of the towering trees, and every now and then we'd break through into a grassy clearing with spectacular views. No one was talking.

Okay, I will now admit that I now sorta "get" the whole nature thing. Don't worry, I'm not going to rush out and buy a backpack or anything. But I will say that being on a horse on top of a mountain made everything seem very small. I felt small, Cosmas seemed small, our perfect fight even seemed smaller. I wondered whether I would ever be able to forget it. Okay, everyone write this down, because it is a very common mistake: It isn't about forgetting, because we all know that takes time, what is needed is remembering the good.

As I watched Cosmas bounce along ahead of me, I remembered that once when we were dating and we went away on vacation I had wanted to go horseback riding but we hadn't gotten around to it. I wasn't really that upset, but I remembered on the plane that I had been thinking about it. As if reading my mind, Cosmas promised that he'd take me horseback riding another time. I remembered how my chest tightened up, how I thought I was going to burst with love and happiness because he was able to read my mind. I remembered thinking that love is a tricky thing and sometimes it's the small things that really matter. I then thought that it's all those small, happy memories **I suddenly felt a little bit better, and I almost smiled.** that fill up one's heart. In fact, I think that's what I told him. I suddenly felt a little bit better, and I almost smiled.

If that was the case, if I started remembering all our great moments, and there were so many, then perhaps I could throw them on top of the remains of the perfect fight and that would put out the smoldering embers. Perhaps they would stack up like bricks and we would start to rebuild. Perhaps the heart was like bone; after it broke it grew back stronger.

Now I know this sounds over-the-top, but it's totally true. Right when I was having this completely profound breakthrough moment, I realized that it had started snowing. It was just a tiny amount, but it was only October, so it was a bit early for snow. I won't even try to describe it except to say it was all very Ansel Adams, but with people. But I did feel it was some sort of sign: "Yes, Jenny. It's about time you started figuring things out."

When we were back in the car and both of us were smiling, it was my turn to make amends by telling him what I had figured out with Shalimar. Just as I was getting started, he asked, "Are you allergic to horses?"

I pulled down the visor to look in the mirror. I was a mess. My face was puffed up, my eyes were tearing, and I started getting itchy all over. Suddenly I was coughing and sneezing. Apparently I *was* allergic to horses—*very* allergic, in fact. So much for my Danielle Steele moment. Cosmas pulled over into the parking lot of a high school and stripped me down outside, handing me the old blanket that was in the trunk. He then dug around in the trunk and got us both a change of clothes; he stripped down and changed and then helped me get dressed again, too, locking all the contaminated stuff in the trunk. Now there really was something to peep at in Vermont. He drove into town in search of a pharmacy. While he was in the drugstore I decided to take another peek at myself. I couldn't believe it; I looked even worse than I did after the fight. Hideous: my eyes were little watery slits, I was all blotchy, my nose was all red and drippy, my face was swollen to almost double its normal size. I decided it was time to invest in expensive eye cream. I was disgusting. Yes, this is exactly how I wanted to look as we made up after our fight—so much for make-up sex. I was sorry for being so awful, and now I looked the part.

I had to take a double dose of Benedryl, and, needless to say, I was pretty incoherent in about fifteen minutes. I had been trying to formulate what I wanted to tell him, but I couldn't manage the right phrasing. I kept opening my mouth, but no words came out. He thought I was suffocating because he pulled over to the side of the road and was about to start CPR.

That was my big chance; it was time to tell him that maybe I was unhappy in Boston only because I never got a chance to spend any time with him, but I wasn't unhappy with him as a husband (though flowers every now and again wouldn't hurt). That maybe I missed my friends and wasn't making any new ones because I wasn't really trying, but that that wasn't his fault. That we were married, and I wanted to be with him no matter where we were (even if the Nieman's in town really was much too small). That the important thing was that I loved him, and that he showed me how much he loved me by saying he was sorry with a weekend in the country and making good on a promise from a long time ago to take me horseback riding. That I now realized one big scary fight didn't mean that our marriage was over, far from it, in fact, because a marriage was over only if we both decided to stop trying, and that one fight, or rather no fight, even a perfect one, would ever make me do that.

Which would then give him the chance to say that by not taking out the trash he wasn't being hostile or show-ing disrespect to me, but that he understood it made me feel that way. He also gave in to the fact that my having to remind/nag him to take out the trash was basically the same thing as having to do it myself, and that he would really, really try not to forget anymore. That maybe he was a bit guilty for taking me for granted and would remember that though I didn't expect a thank-you for the things I did, it would be nice on his part to toss one out (like with flowers) every now and again. And lastly, that even though he was at a crucial stage in his career and I had been very, very understanding about it for many, *many* years (med school, residency, and now his first year of fellowship), he had also realized that we were in a crucial stage in our marriage and that I needed some of his time and attention as well.

But as I finally opened my mouth to speak, he said it all for both of us. Honing in on exactly what I had been thinking, he said, "I had a really great weekend, too. Let's go leaf peeping every year."

I just smiled, nodded, and passed out.

CHAPTER SIX

To Love, Honor, and Cherish

DOUBLE DATING, DOUBLE TROUBLE

Cosmas came bursting through the door, breezed right past me sitting at the kitchen table, and walked into the bedroom where he began calling out my name in a very excited and very *loud* tone. "Sweetheart, I'm home! Where are you? I've got great news!" I stood up and tapped him on the shoulder from behind, and he turned and pulled me into his arms. I got a big furry kiss on the cheek. (Cosmas had the beginning of a beard, and we were engaged in a weeklong debate about whether he should keep going or shave it off.) I naturally assumed that his joyful mood meant that he had just managed to isolate some new protein or had just found a matching DNA sequence string for the new gene he was working on. Of course, I don't really understand what any of these things mean, and he has certainly tried to explain them to me a few times, but I am a classic English major who is really clueless when it comes to science. Even if I had taken more science in college, it wouldn't have mattered; Cosmas is way beyond college science. When other little boys were reading comic books or collecting baseball cards, he had been reading *Scientific American* and memorizing the periodic chart. It used to bother me a little bit, that I couldn't fully share in his work victories and problems, but I have since realized that it wasn't anything that I could change, and I have settled for being happy when he's happy, regardless of whether I know what the hell it was that made him that way.

His excitement made me giddy, too, and suddenly I was begging, "Tell me, tell me, tell me," and was dancing around in front of him, squealing like a schoolgirl who just had a cute boy ask her out. And, lo and behold, what do I find out? Well, that *he* had just been asked out on a date by a cute boy, or rather, *we* had just been asked out by the most popular doctor couple in the department! He set the scene for me: He was reading the latest issue of *Nature Genetics* (think *People* but for hard-core geeks) while eating lunch in the cafeteria when Dr. James Dean (his real name) slid into the seat across from him and they proceeded to "shoot the breeze for a full eleven minutes and twenty-eight seconds." I just smiled at this, thinking how it was cute that he had timed it, and I made a mental note to sit down and teach him some updated lingo phrases for social interaction, I mean, who still says "shooting the breeze"?

We had just been asked out by the most popular doctor couple in the department!

Dr. James Dean was a few years Cosmas's senior and can best be described as the classic "popular guy." Everybody knew him. Everybody liked him. And just like high school, everybody wanted to eat lunch with him. I remembered hearing all about James when Cosmas first started working. James told such a funny joke. James was always making the nurses blush. James did this. James did that. James, James, James. So when I finally met him I was expecting Russell Crowe with a colonoscope, but what I realized was that everything is relative . . . and what's "super cool" in the world of science and medicine (think of all the science nerds from high school all grown up and wearing white lab coats) was just "pretty cool" in the rest of the world, so let's just say he's no George Clooney. I mean, Dr. James Dean certainly seemed like a great guy—good-looking, easy laugh, and fun to talk to, but as I explained to Cosmas later, Dr. Dean was interesting to talk to mainly because he didn't talk about hospital stuff all the time. He talked about "normal" things like books, movies, and politics, as opposed to the properties of liver enzymes and advantages of gastric bypasses.

Anyway, Cosmas had only eaten with James in the company of other colleagues; he had never been singled out by him before. So, long story short, James had said that he and his wife were going to be in the city on Saturday night and asked whether we wanted to get together for drinks or dinner. Cosmas admitted that he had almost choked on his milk when he heard this, but luckily he had remained calm and even pretended for 8.2 seconds to think about whether or not we had plans (not even close, as I have declared time and time again that walking to the video store does not fit the requirements of an "evening out"). So this was when Cosmas told me that James and his wife, Kendra, were coming over to our apartment on Saturday night at seven P.M. for cocktails and then we'd go to dinner somewhere local. My eyes got a little big at this point because it was now Thursday evening, the apartment was a wreck, and all we had in the fridge were Diet Cokes and frozen French-bread pizzas, which, last time I checked, had not made the Martha Stewart top-ten list of classy hors d'oeuvres.

This was when I tried to clarify things, careful not to burst Cosmas's bubble. So what I thought was, YOU DID

WHAT? YOU INVITED THEM HERE? ARE YOU MAD? But what I said was, "Honeybear, couldn't we just meet them at the restaurant? Don't you think that would be better?" Having them come here entailed a lot of work on our part (translation: my part); someone would have to buy liquor (me), someone would have to buy cheese and crackers (me), and then we'd have to spend an hour or two cleaning up the apartment (this would be an actual we, because there was no way I was going to get stuck doing that all by myself).

He looked crestfallen, and I felt instantly chagrined because Cosmas was not the most social guy you've ever met, and I was always encouraging him to be more social whenever possible. So I did a quick 180 and completely changed my tone—I told him I was just kidding, that I'd love to have the famous Dr. James over for cocktails, and that I'd make sure everything was just perfect. I then reminded him that I thought he was just as cool as Dr. Dean, and he was certainly cuter. Cosmas gave me this look that said, "Okay, I'm probably on the same cute level (though James worked out), but as far as being cool, not a chance in hell." This is where I explained to him that in the land of married couples, there was a group scoring on the coolness factor, and our combined score was definitely on the level with Dr. James and his wife, well, unless he was married to a Rhodes scholar supermodel.

I stayed true to my word. I cleaned the apartment. I stocked the fridge with vodka, tonic, limes, beer, lemon-ade, OJ, and soda. I bought four types of cheese, three types of berries, melon—which I carved into little balls—six different-shaped crackers, two different types of dips, and cocktail napkins with little witticisms printed on them (they sound tacky, but they weren't). I researched ice sculptures, but you needed three days' advanced notice.

Meanwhile, Cosmas went out and got his hair cut, had the car washed in case we drove them to dinner, and spent an hour trying to figure out what to wear. Every few minutes he would come out of the bedroom and hold up various shirts and pants. In the end he decided on his dark khaki pants, and the top three shirt choices included his Burberry denim shirt, his pale blue Lacoste long-sleeve shirt, or a slate blue silk cashmere—blend sweater shirt that I bought him for his last birthday. I could tell he wanted to wear the denim shirt because he spent the most time in front of the mirror with that one, but something was bothering him about it; I recognized the look of its not being perfect enough. It was the same look we women wear when we have on a low-cut top and wish we had bigger boobs, the look of knowing that a skirt would look a little better if our calves were a bit thinner, the look of wishing we could just lose those last ten pounds. I asked him what was wrong, and he told me that the shirt was a little wrinkled. Okay, obviously his look was a bit different from a female's, because women tend to obsess about things that can't be fixed. So I offered to iron it for him. He gave me a look of such gratitude that it sort of creeped me out. It soon turned to a look of suspicion, probably over the fact that he didn't think I knew how to iron. I grabbed the shirt from him and said, "Just because I don't iron doesn't mean I can't iron!"

I cleaned the apartment. I stocked the fridge with vodka, tonic, limes, beer, lemonade, OJ, and soda. I bought four types of cheese.

As I ironed we moved on to the next really big decision, which was to shave or not to shave. We formed a huddle to discuss. Cosmas laid out the facts. James was very put together and always clean-shaven, so shaving seemed like a no-brainer, until you considered the fact that Cosmas looks a little older and more rugged with a few days' growth. I told him not to shave but to trim up a bit so it was more scruff than fur. He then spent the next forty minutes in the bathroom trimming it with little scissors. He was dressed and ready two hours before they were even expected to arrive, so he turned his nervous energy toward me and politely inquired into what I was planning to wear.

Okay, enough was enough. I had not said one word about all the craziness up until now. I recognized that there was definitely some Freudian stuff at work here, because Cosmas never hung out with the popular crowd growing up, and even though one would think he's way past all that, such memories die hard. So I got it, but that didn't give him the right to fixate on what I was going to wear. Those were not my issues, and when it came to clothes, I was more than capable of dressing for any occasion (though I had overshot twice in Boston by being way overdressed for the occasion, in New York City there was no such thing). So I glared at him. "You want to know what exactly?" I gave a look that said he should probably take this opportunity to back down, especially since I just spent my entire Saturday shopping and cleaning. He backed down, and I sent him to the local Starbucks to chill out and read a nonscience magazine so he could brush up on his current events.

They were right on time, which threw me in a panic as no one I knew (except myself) was ever on time. I thought I would have a few more minutes to prep him before they showed up. Good thing we lived in a walk-up. I started telling him that the best way to greet them would be to follow their lead in terms of touching (hand shake versus the American air kiss or the European air kiss, etc.). I said I would take their coats, and he would lead them to the living room. He was then supposed to find out what they would like to drink (man's job), and I'd bring out the fruit plate that was chilling in the fridge. I reminded him to be himself—well, to be himself but in a less science-y way. I reminded him that we had recently gone to a friend's wedding and he could share an anecdote from that, that we had seen a movie the night before, and that he had found some interesting stuff while reading his magazine. I told him if we got into any awkward pauses or weird silences, he was immediately to withdraw and I'd jump in and handle the situation.

Cocktails went off beautifully, they loved the spread, and they clued in to all the bait that I had left around . . . our wedding and honeymoon picture on the windowsill, which led right into when we all got married, where we went on our respective honeymoons, etc. The men talked about work for a while, and Kendra and I talked about girlie stuff. When we hit a brief lull, James picked up the second piece of bait, which was the current controversial literary fiction book

When we hit a brief lull, James picked up the second piece of bait.

that was on the bestseller list and was sitting on our coffee table right in front of him, which veered the conversation into reading tastes. Cosmas was able to say that he had read last year's Pulitzer Prize–winning novel, without having to admit that I filled him in on the ending because he had read only half of it and that it was the only book he had "read" in the past year. When we launched into movies, I knew we'd be fine; Cosmas and I saw everything, and he spoke quite eloquently about special effects and action sequences. So far so good.

Finally, it was time to leave for dinner; by then everyone was jovial and talking loudly, and it seemed totally comfortable. As we were walking toward the car, Cosmas whispered, "Do you think they like us?" I nodded yes and told him, "I never thought that they wouldn't." We went to a rowdy and popular tapas place for dinner, somewhere that Cosmas and I had gone before, so we knew that the food was good. (Why risk an evening by trying out a new restaurant—on first dates, it's better to go with the tried-and-true.)

At dinner we discussed recent and future vacations, in-laws, the economy, poker, meat-loaf recipes, hospital gossip, and the fact that none of us was quite ready for children. I had watched everyone carefully; no one ever checked his or her watch, and the dinner went on for over two hours. We parted after midnight with everyone saying what a good time they had and promises to get together again soon. The women air kissed (European style) and the men did that thing where they gave each other a hearty handshake (using both hands) but you could tell they would have liked to have hugged.

When we got back home and started cleaning up, I taught Cosmas how to deconstruct a date to find out whether it was successful or not. I explained that first there needed to be more similarities than differences between us as couples—well, first and foremost, we obviously had the doctor thing going for us. We also had the fact that they had gotten married around the same time and weren't quite ready for kids. I had us covered on reading preferences, and Cosmas shared Kendra's interest in antiques. The biggest positive in my opinion was that they had both lived in New York City at some point, a major bonding point for me. So far, no real glaring differences, except that they lived outside Boston, but that was due to necessity not choice.

The second indicator was that everyone seemed to laugh a lot and that both parties shared engaging and interesting stories. We got a thumbs-up on that one, as again it was pretty evenly split with Dr. James and me having the biggest mouths.

Lastly, the surefire best way to judge how the evening went was by number of "future projections," meaning how often did someone project us all into the future by saying things like, "We should all go see that photography exhibit at the MFA that's coming next month, it's supposed to be amazing"; or "We've been dying to try that new restaurant, too, we should all go sometime soon," etc. I had counted at least four such projectionary statements during the course of our evening (anything over three was really good), which meant that odds were, one of them should come to fruition. By my guidelines, we determined that the entire evening was close to a 5.8 on the Olympic scale.

Each evening for the following week, when Cosmas came home from work, I asked him whether or not he had run into Dr. Dean in the hallway or in the cafeteria. I was dying to know what they had thought of our evening out—did he seem to be friendlier than before? And the best-case scenario would be that he would seek Cosmas out and make a second date right on the spot. Cosmas said he hadn't seen him at all, and at first this didn't faze me because Cosmas is not the most observant fellow in

Had we come on too strong? Were we too aggressive? Could we have scared them off somehow?

the world. After a week of this, I was convinced that something was wrong—the hospital wasn't that big and they hadn't mentioned any trips that they were about to take. What if Dr. Dean had seen Cosmas but was purposely avoiding him? Maybe I had been dead wrong and they hadn't had a good time with us. Had we come on too strong? Were we too aggressive? Could we have scared them off somehow? Perhaps I overdid it with the three different types of berries. I cursed the fact that I always had to overdo everything. I knew I should have asked Mary Sunshine for a batch of her stupid onion dip; that would have certainly secured a second date—but no, I had wanted to do it on my own.

Cosmas finally grew tired of my pestering him about it and suggested that perhaps we should call them. I flat out refused. We were the girl in this scenario; we couldn't call first. No, the ball was definitely in their court. Cosmas asked how we ended up being the "girl" in the relationship, and I told him that since the Deans asked us out first, that made them the guy. Besides, we're the ones who had spent hours getting ready for it—and that *definitely* made us the girl. Normally, being the girl shouldn't be a big deal, because obviously I'd been one all my life and knew that I had been an all-star player in the dating games. In fact, I can't remember one single time when I went out on a first date and didn't get asked out again, which is, of course, why I found our current situation so incredibly frustrating and perplexing.

One thing I didn't understand was why Cosmas didn't seem to mind one way or another; it made no sense because he was the one who had a big crush on Dr. Dean to begin with. What happened to James, James, James? Delicately I inquired about this. I said, "Doesn't it bother you that we haven't been asked out again?" He just sort of shrugged and said that he hadn't thought about it that much. I pressed him on the subject, and he started to get annoyed. Then he told me that he had had fun with them and that he was positive they had had a good time with us as well. He reasoned that we were all busy and said that he was sure we'd all get together again sometime in the future. Ahhhh, then I got it; even though we were the girl in this dating situation, Cosmas was still thinking like a guy, and he obviously seemed fine with the whole thing, even if it turned out to be just a one-night stand. He had gotten everything he wanted—a night out on the town with James—another notch in the belt, a new entry in his social C.V. Well, for me, the one-night stand scenario was totally unacceptable; I had invested an entire Saturday of my time. I needed a little ROI (return on investment)—by God, I wanted to get on their holiday card list, and I wanted to put them on mine.

I knew it was up to me to start plotting out the next course of action, and if I had to do it alone, then so be it. Over dinner the next few nights I began subtly to ask about the other doctors in the department—who seemed to be friends with whom, and that kind of thing. Did anyone live near one another? Who had kids and who didn't? What sorts of cars did everyone drive? Finally, I got the nugget of info that I was looking for, the fact that James played racquetball with a few of the other doctors in the department. From those names I finally extracted the best choice for my plan; apparently one of the doctors whom James played with was married, about our age, and lived somewhat near us. I asked Cosmas whether he thought Dr. Sampson and James were friends. He thought he had maybe seen them eat lunch together once or twice, but he didn't know for sure. So I then suggested to Cosmas that we should ask them out to dinner—perhaps starting with drinks at our place again (this time I was definitely going to have the dip). Cosmas agreed and didn't even question my sudden new interest in socializing with his colleagues when I had never seemed interested before. This was fine by me, as all would become clear in due time.

The Sampsons agreed to a dinner, and this time it was I who was nervous and fanatical about every single detail— the apartment was spotless; I bought new wineglasses; not only did we have Mary Sunshine's famous onion party dip but I had asked for her help artfully arranging everything. I had always wondered who bought all those kitchen gadgets you see on late-night television, and now I realized it was other suburban legends like her (probably because I bet she never sleeps). She had a gunlike thing that pressed my three different cheeses into cute shapes. The sweet red pepper hummus was overflowing out of a butternut squash that had been carved to look like a volcano, and the fruit platter, well, the sheer beauty of it almost made me weep. She insisted that I take the credit for everything, and I told her that I owed her a big one for all her help. She said that she was happy to help, and besides, it wasn't as if our relationship was one-sided because she was very grateful to me for helping her find and convincing her to buy a pair of black leather pants (her husband was even more thankful).

Cosmas still hadn't noticed that anything was amiss and was just happy that I hadn't asked for his help with anything so far. There was a *Law and Order* marathon on TV, and he had happily spent the whole afternoon on the couch yelling out to me his guesses for the real culprit. Ninety minutes before they were supposed to arrive I made him go and change, and I casually handed him a set of index cards. He looked at them and then at me. I tried to be casual about it and suggested that he flip through them and memorize as much as he could before tonight. I watched him carefully as he shuffled through my flash cards of the "entertaining cocktail conversation" facts and stories that I had outlined for him. It was just a few interesting facts about the history of racquetball, suggested compliments about the high ratings and reviews that *Consumer Reports* had given the car that they drove (well, if Cosmas was right that he drove a red 1999 Volvo sedan), and the top-five personal couple anecdotes that I felt Cosmas was good at telling. He looked up from the cards and gave me a quizzical look, then asked me what was going on because this didn't seem like a fun dinner with one of his colleagues (yes, Cosmas was the third brother of the Hardy boys, the one who didn't make the cut).

I told him that I just wanted tonight to be fun, that was all, and that I was just being proactive in terms of ensuring the success of the evening. Cosmas went into the kitchen and stopped short when he saw the volcano. He told me that the food was too much, that they were going to think we were freaks. I informed him that Mary had helped me with it and that as soon as they tasted the food, they would be totally at our mercy and would fall in love with my culinary displays of Hawaii (Mary had used one of the volcanoes in Hawaii as her model). Besides, hadn't he told me that he had overheard that they had just returned from vacationing in Hawaii?

He then gave me a look that said that I needed to come clean and let him know what was really going on, because he always knew that I was a little crazy, but this was bordering on Tonya Harding.

So I told him—explaining that if he could just play along for the night we'd make sure that this was the absolute best double date of their lives. That when Dr. Sampson played racquetball with Dr. Dean next week, James would surely ask about his weekend and Dr. Sampson would gush about how much fun they'd had with us—about the dip, the other food, and the many funny stories we had to share—and upon hearing all about it, Dr. Dean would—

"Is that what this is all about? Are you trying to make Dr. Dean jealous?"

Cosmas blurted it out, "Is that what this is all about? Are you trying to make Dr. Dean jealous?"

Hell, yeah. I told him that I was deeply offended that they hadn't called us to ask us out again. That I wasn't about to let anyone use us for a one-night stand, and that we were about to dethrone Dr. Dean and his wife as the most popular couple in the department. Then I started quoting the movie *Gladiator* about how once you won the crowd over you would have the power. It was probably one of my best Lady Macbeth moments.

Cosmas burst out laughing at this, and then told me that, oh, by the way, hadn't he mentioned that he had run into James the other day at one of the weekly meetings? It turned out that James was currently doing a rotation at a different hospital, which was why he hadn't been around, and that he and Kendra had had a really great time with us. James had also complimented the melon balls and fruit platter that I had served, and he said that they had some relatives coming to visit over the next few weeks, but as soon as the relatives were gone, James and Kendra wanted to ask us over to their house for dinner.

I was stunned. Suddenly all my grandiose plans did seem a bit like Brenda on 90210. Of course, there was a logical explanation about why we hadn't heard from them after our date last month. Wow, dinner at their house . . . hmmm, that meant that they really liked us; I was sure that dinner at home was probably like skipping second base and going straight to third—not bad, not bad at all.

My thoughts now moved to the current situation; this late-breaking news sort of changed things a bit. Now my plan could potentially backfire because Dr. Dean might hear that we served up food that was even better than the stupid little melon balls we had served them. What if they took it as a sign that we were more interested in this new couple than in them? Worse yet, what if they thought we were fickle and weren't really looking for a committed relationship—that maybe we were just interested in playing the field—that we were . . . sluts.

I was snapped back from my thoughts by Cosmas jumping up and down with joy. He must have just discovered the Mary Sunshine pie that I had hidden away in one of the cupboards. That was going to be my heavy artillery, only to be brought out if we needed the help. I knew we probably wouldn't need it since the dip would certainly suffice, but then again, lactose intolerance was on the rise these days, so I had erred on the side of caution. Well, I certainly wasn't going to serve it now, because we certainly didn't want them to fall head over heels for us; on the other hand, we were the guy in the relationship, and this may very well turn out to be a one-night stand, then we might as well give them the night of their lives, right?

Hmmmm, being the guy was not bad, not bad at all.

MAKING TIME FOR NEW AND FUN

I have always been a bit hyperactive. When I was younger (six or seven or thereabouts) my mother and the mother of my then-best friend, Adam Thompson, decided that they might have some hope of maintaining a sliver of their sanity if they packaged us together and took turns watching us after school. I always knew whether it was my mom's turn or not by her demeanor in the morning. If she was bright and cheery, that meant it was not her turn. If she was on her third cup of coffee and looking as if she'd kill for a cigarette even though she never smoked in her life, that meant it was her turn. They were not doling out Ritalin like candy in those days, so whoever had us for the afternoon had to prepare herself for a high-octane extravaganza. It probably would have been okay if we had been loud and messy yet somewhat contained, but we were loud and messy heat-seeking missiles of everything and anything that was new and fun—making mud pies, digging up anthills, starting an ant farm with empty jars, playing mad scientists who mixed potions of whatever we found in the fridge, being painters, being painters who used their feet, acting out cowboys and cowboys or Indians and Indians (we were in that phase where we both wanted to be on the same side), and pretending to be botanists who were able to raze a flower bed in four minutes flat. And that would be just one afternoon.

I think my mother still blamed Adam for my inability to stick with one thing and my constant hunger for the new and fun. She had told me time and time again that life was not all about new and fun. I told her that I knew that, but could you blame me for trying? So now twenty or so years later I was still what is known as a "phaser." Just a smattering of my phases: darts (three months, spent $150 on set of darts); pool (on and off for five years, spent $500 on pool cue); karate (two sessions, paid for ten); boxing (five lessons, own five pairs of red boxing shorts—there was a sale); pottery (one hour, couldn't deal with the clay under my nails); yoga; ice-skating; poker; video games; origami; Rollerblading; bonsai tree sculpting; bicycling; soccer (bought a ball but never played); knitting (made four hats and own eight different-size needles); and bowling. In fact, I couldn't think of one thing that I have started and stayed committed to, other than reading, writing, shopping, and breathing. For whatever reason I didn't really worry about my capricious personality too much when it came to marriage, because I had really run the gamut from being a single girl, to a single girl who dated tons of guys, to a single girl in relationships with the wrong guys, to a single girl who swore off men, and

For whatever reason I didn't really worry about my capricious personality too much when it came to marriage.

finally a single girl who tried everything else and was finally ready to settle down with Mr. Right.

In the beginning of our marriage, everything was new and fun—going grocery shopping, folding laundry, waking up on a Saturday morning, even cleaning the bathroom (water fights would always be fun). Even things that sound dreadful, like going to the hardware store to buy a shade for the bathroom window, we found new and fun.

Then slowly things began to settle down: routines were established; chores that were once done together were now divided up and done alone. We soon tapped out all the restaurants within walking distance; the video-store clerk knew me by name, and every now and again I'd wake up on a Saturday morning and, for the tiniest little second, "Oh, you're still here," zipped across my brain. Hello, monotony. At first I didn't understand what I was feeling because I had never before had fixed schedules and routines. So I described my sluggishness to Stephanie, one of my best friends, and asked her whether she thought I had chronic fatigue syndrome. She said that I wasn't sick but that I sounded bored. I railed at the thought, totally horrified, and I grew instantly defensive. She told me to calm down because she wasn't saying that I was boring (my worst nightmare), rather that I was bored. She remarked that it had been a while since I'd had a new "project" or "phase." I told her that I had gotten married, and she informed me that as far as she knew marriage was neither a project nor a phase.

So when Cosmas and I were eating dinner later that evening, I asked him if he was bored. He told me no and then let me know that I wasn't either. He told me we were both so busy with work all the time we barely even saw each other, so how could we be bored? I told him that I was worried about monotony in our marriage and that I thought we needed to be more proactive and work against it. He said fine by him as long as I took it on as a project because he didn't have time. I thought about what he said and knew he was right in a way, because it wasn't as if we were ever sitting and staring out of a window with nothing to do; in fact, we always complained about having too much to do. I decided to investigate the matter further.

After careful thought and extensive observation (two weeks, I worked fast), I came to the conclusion that time is a very tricky issue when it comes to marriage; in fact, I think it's a catch-22. So the facts were that we never seemed to have enough time, since work kept us both extremely busy, and then we had the chores/life-maintenance issues that also took up a lot of time. So what got shortchanged in all of this was our quality time as a couple.

A running joke I had with my husband was that there were only two times when we got to see each other every day—eleven P.M. and six A.M. Suddenly we'd find ourselves alone and together in the same room, and we'd check our watches or glance at a clock; yep, it's eleven P.M. And one if not both of us desperately needed to go to sleep because we had an early morning meeting, or because we'd had only four hours of sleep the night before. Or it was six A.M.—the alarm had already been snoozed three times, and we were all warm in bed where we could so easily hang out (and even have sex), but one if not both of us needed to get up and get started with another long and busy day.

This quandary got us every time because, of course, part of us always wanted to spend a little time together and just powwow, catch up with each other's lives and careers. But nine times out of ten, we seemed to let those moments go, because one if not both of us decided that we would catch up with each other tomorrow, or the day after, or maybe over the weekend. So we borrowed against our together time to make up for the lack of time we had for everything else. It was easy to rationalize this decision because we figured we could always make it up on the back end since we were going to be married forever, right? And there was a lot of extra time in forever.

After we did everything that we needed to do, we'd see if there was anything left over; if so, then we would spend that time together. Inevitably, we were tired during these times—our long-awaited chance to relax, so we got into the habit of staying in and renting movies, ordering food, and watching TV. Boring.

I started trying to break some of these patterns. I tried out new rules—no watching TV when we eat, no matter how tired we were (unless *The West Wing* is on, of course). No talking about bills over dinner, or about what we ate for lunch. No wearing clothes at the table (he vetoed this one, so I can't tell you whether that one would work). And, of course, that tried-and-true prescription for a healthy marriage—I swear everyone gives the same advice; I heard it from my mom, his mom, our priest, my sister-in-law, and married and single friends alike—the great institution of Date Night.

I was going to start dating—it could be with him or with someone else.

At first it was hard to take Date Night seriously, or rather it was hard for Cosmas to take it seriously, and, in fact, I pointedly told him that if we hadn't already been married, I would have dumped his ass long ago for constantly calling me and canceling (I mean, I knew he was busy at the hospital, but look at *ER*, they all seem to have the time to date and have sex). My new stance (stance, threat, call it whatever you want) was letting him know in the simplest possible terms that I was going to start dating—it could be with him or with someone else.

He was late picking me up for our very first date and was a little surprised to see me dressed up and smelling good; and I had even hot-rolled my hair. So I was all excited, because just getting ready made me feel all festive. (I used to spend a good two hours getting ready when I was single, dancing around my apartment to early Madonna.)

"So Mr. Hot Date, where are you taking me?" I asked coyly.

He paused a moment too long and did that thing with his neck where he sort of stretched it out, and I knew he hadn't made any plans at all. He tried to cover by saying that he'd take me anywhere I wanted to go, but he could tell by the way I was flexing my jaw that he was busted. Well, we certainly weren't going to get in anywhere good without a reservation on a Friday night, so that didn't leave us with many options. I tried not to get upset, because maybe I hadn't explained to him that Date Night meant a real date, where real plans had to be made. We ended up at a local Thai place and afterward, when he asked me if I wanted to go to a bar or to a movie, I said I didn't feel up to it. I told him I had a headache. Right after I said it, I freaked out, because I didn't really have a headache at all. What was happening? Was I turning into one of those bored, dissatisfied wives who always had a headache and who sat around and waited for the mailman to deliver her *TV Guide* each week so she could highlight the shows she wanted to watch?

When he went out to get bagels the next morning, he came back with flowers. Instead of making me feel better, this only made me feel worse. This routine probably dates back to the Stone Age. Man screws up. Woman gets pissed. Man gives flowers. Little stick figure representations etched into the cave wall from the Paleolithic period. Before we got married I got the I-love-you-and-can't-stop-thinking-about-you flowers. These were I'm-sorry-that-I-didn't-think-enough-about-you flowers. I told him that I didn't want I'm-sorry flowers in the future.

Date two was a big improvement. Of course I got flowers, but I knew I would since men are so predictable in that way. He took me on one of those dinner-dance cruises that you always see advertised when you're single and that sound like so much fun but seem more like a married-person type of activity. Well, it is a married

person type of activity—married for like fifty-plus years—
we were one of the youngest couples there. Cosmas told
me that one of the senior doctors had told him about it
(well, at least it wasn't golf lessons). I decided not to let it
get to me, because I never really expected Cosmas to show
up in a leather-and-spandex ensemble and take me out
to clubs that were filled with tons of young lithe girls
gyrating around the dance floor in Britney-wear.

What we needed for date three was to find something
that worked for our own age bracket, post—*St. Elmo's Fire*
(remember how they were all looking through the windows at the college bar/hangout and decided that it was
time they moved on to a more mature venue?), heck
maybe even post-*Friends* (or at least a fatter version), but
way before *Everybody Loves Raymond*. Together we racked our
brains, which entailed my pouring through the *Improper
Bostonian* for ideas while Cosmas read the *Wall Street Journal*
and said "Mmm-huh" and "That sounds nice" to whatever I mentioned. I decided that it came down to a
numbers game (same principle when single and dating—
the more you date, the more free dinners and the better
the odds of finding "the one"); we just had to try as may
new things as possible to find the right glass slipper that
was going to fit our collective foot and transform us into
an exciting and magical couple. Ballroom dancing? Nah,

that was probably not the best idea, just ask any of our 175 wedding guests who saw us flail our way through Sinatra's "Fly Me to the Moon" during our wedding reception. Sailing? Ugh, too messy—the combination of wind and lip gloss was a big no-no. Triathalon training? I just threw that one out to see if Cosmas was listening. (He wasn't, so he had to cook and do the dishes as punishment, so there.) Friday night cooking classes at the Cambridge Adult Center? Hmmm, that one was a definite maybe as it could be fun and useful (I love multitasking) regarding our dinner rut, but I'd have to call ahead and find out about the issue of clean-up—no way was I doing dishes on a date. Pottery painting? Nope. Camping? Nope. Karaoke? I wish, but neither of us can carry a tune. Perhaps lip synching? I began to realize that it wasn't going to be as easy to transform into one of those "couples that do fun things" as I had originally thought.

The tricky part was figuring out the things that both of us would be interested in doing, and what made my situation Mission Impossible 3 was the fact that Cosmas really didn't have any hobbies, nor did he seem to want any. Whenever I inquired about such things with him, he would tell me the same thing: "I have work and I have you. I'm not interested in anything else. You're my hobby." I must admit I had always found his one-track mind very flattering, and I wasn't sure why all of a sudden I was convinced that we were the most boring couple on the planet. It was probably due to seeing other couples out on the street who always seemed to be doing these fun couple-y things together—going on picnics (ugh, bugs), checking out the festivals at the Charles River

The tricky part was figuring out the things that both of us would be interested in doing.

(no way, too many people), antiquing (maybe, if you held a gun to my head), as if doing those things made them a better couple than us on the master couple scoreboard in the sky.

I mean, it's not as if Cosmas and I never did anything together as a couple—in fact, I'd put big money down on the fact that no couple could beat us when it came to going to the movies. In that area of our lives, I was sure that we were on par with any couple that has celebrated a silver or golden anniversary. Definitely gold medalist contenders for the GACO Olympics. We were like mind readers when it came to our weekend movie outings, barely needing to say more than ten words to each other—perfectly in sync in every way. I checked the times, he picked me up (Cosmas was never late for the movies); I bought tickets while he parked the car. He got the concessions while I aggressively scoured for the perfect seats (close, but not too close; not behind anyone who didn't seem like polite movie slouchers; always on the aisle for easy access to refills and bathroom); I held the popcorn during the previews (he needed all his concentration for this, his favorite part); he held it during the first half; and if there was any left (doubtful), he'd hand off to me when he went to the bathroom during the middle of the movie. (Time and time again I tell him to pace his soda intake during the first half of the movie.) I'd mouth a few choice words to catch him up, and, like a code cracker, he'd know exactly what he'd missed; we even had all the hand-holding positions down pat so that neither one of our arms would go to sleep. At the end of the movie we'd both jump up (unless it was one of the credits with bloopers at the end), and I would expertly snake our way up the aisle in record time, with Cosmas's hands around my waist and his making "ssssss" noises in my ear. We were that good. I smiled, and suddenly I felt a little better. Okay, maybe we weren't at the top of the heap when it came to exciting married couples, but we weren't at the bottom of it, either. I guess we had our things (we were equally skilled in video stores as well), and other couples had theirs.

So what I learned was that once you got married, you couldn't always expect everything to be new and fun, but as a pair it might be wise to at least strive toward one of those two attributes. So we decided (or, rather, I decided—same difference, though) that we would trade off and I would be in charge of any new thing that we could try together as a couple (excluding all extreme sports, as Cosmas said that his Mountain Dew days were probably already behind him), and Cosmas would be in charge of the old standby fun things that we could do together (like seeing movies). So if we tried something new and it happened to be fun, too, then Cosmas could take that activity and add it into his rotation, but if we tried something new and one of us hated it (like antiquing), then we would just cross it off the list. May not work for everyone, but it works for us.

LOVE STORY II: THE SEQUEL

Most of the time it's easier to let it go, be wise, and pick your battles carefully, but then there were the days when I just had to ask, Why? Sometimes, when the injustice was just too great, just too in my face—so close I could smell its Nacho Cheese Doritos breath—I just had to say some thing.

It started with a simple question, "Wasn't that *Love Story* a few channels back?" I felt him shift his weight ever so slightly, and suddenly his channel flipping rhythm was totally off. I watched him close his eyes a moment longer than a blink, and in my mind's eye I pictured his mind's eye, which was probably seeing a shadowy figure (him) as it ran screaming down a long dark corridor. I got a mmmm-like noise, which turned into a semi-sigh and finally ended up in a "Oh, was it?" that was one octave higher than his normal voice. Cosmas was the worst liar ever.

"Wasn't that *Love Story* a few channels back?"

I told him that, yes, it most certainly was the movie *Love Story* now some ten channels back, on channel 25 to be exact, and that it had started only about twenty minutes ago—it was at the part where they had already had sex but before and only minutes from the great snowy falling-in-love montage. He asked how I managed to figure that out in the five seconds before he changed the channel. I corrected him; it had, in fact, been only two and a half seconds, and I accused him of reducing his usual five seconds per channel in the hopes that I wouldn't notice what was playing. I squeezed his arm and told him that I was sure it was an unconscious act on his part, something hardwired into all male brains, perhaps.

So then I asked him if he'd like to watch it with me. He said sure, but hadn't we just watched it a few weeks ago? I couldn't help but do a snortlike laugh at this because it hadn't been weeks ago since we had last seen it together. No, it had been years ago—six years and, oh, I'd say about two months—and that was the first and only time he had ever seen it. It was late one Tuesday evening, and we were sitting on his couch in his New York apartment; he was flipping channels much the same way he had just been doing when I noticed that *Love Story* was on, and I squealed with delight. That time he had immediately flipped back to it and asked what I was so happy about. I realized then that he was a *Love Story* virgin.

Since it had already begun, I insisted that we go out right then and there and rent it. There were certain reference points that a person has in her life, and I needed all of my quotes from *Love Story* to be fully recognized and understood. At the time we had been dating for only a few months and were still in the fantastic gaga stage when he'd do anything and everything I wanted, so he was all for watching it, and unless he was once a good liar, I think he really enjoyed it. (Unfortunately, I'm not at liberty to say whether or not he cried at the end, because I promised I wouldn't tell—but c'mon, you'd have to have a heart like stone not to.)

We could have continued with our little verbal foxtrot, but I decided to take a novel approach by being direct and simply asking him why he couldn't watch *Love Story* again, for only the second time, when I had graciously watched *Die Hard 2* all 17 million times it has been aired on TBS. He said he would love to watch *Love Story* again, but he knew that I had seen it 19 million times and so he wasn't sure whether I'd wanted to see it again, especially since I missed the beginning (I was a stickler about having to see things from the beginning). He tried a diversionary tactic and offered to rent it over the weekend. Nice try, buddy, but if he thought I would fall for the old maybe-if-I-put-it-off-until-the-weekend-she-would-forget-about-it trick, then he was wrong.

I could have let the whole thing go at that point because we were now watching it—Cosmas flipped back to it after I stared at him unblinking for like three minutes; luckily we were just in time for the snow scene—but I didn't. I really wanted to understand why he didn't want to watch it again when he had told me before that he really liked it the first time around. So I asked, and he shrugged. I took the remote from him and muted the sound (I know practically every line in the movie), and again I inquired why he could watch the *Matrix* a hundred times (I had once seen him watch back-to-back airings) but not this movie twice. Again, I got a shrug. I upped the ante and told him that if he could make me understand his "guy logic," we wouldn't have to watch the rest of the movie that night.

I observed him considering my offer, first trying to decide whether it was some sort of trap that would ultimately have him watching Lifetime movies for the next week, or whether I was being aboveboard. I held up three fingers and said on 007's honor I was being serious and that this wasn't some sort of trap. Whenever I read his mind like that he gets a funny look on his face and burrows deeper into the couch, like Godzilla grabbing for the power lines, hoping to gather a bit more strength. Now he knew that I knew that his feelings for James Bond were very serious and that I would never take 007's name in vain out of respect for him, which proved I was legit. He took a deep breath, and I leaned forward in anticipation of this revolutionary new knowledge; he then said that he honestly had never thought about why he could enjoy multiple viewings of *Mission Impossible 2*, anything with Chow Yun Fat in it (except for *Anna and the King*), and *Cliffhanger*, to name just a few favorites, while he had absolutely no desire whatsoever to watch *Love Story*, *About Last Night*, and *Pretty Woman* even a second time, despite having enjoyed them once.

He had on a smug look of satisfaction when he grabbed for the remote. WAS HE FOR REAL? All he had done was put his shrug into sentence form; he hadn't answered the question at all. I refused to let go of the remote, and I let him know that though I certainly appreciated his gut-wrenching honesty in the matter, he had to do a little more soul-searching to make me really understand. He rolled his eyes, sighed, and sort of slumped a bit in defeat; his hand twitched a little from remote withdrawal. I told him that lately I had been in the mood to watch one of my other all-time favorite movies,

He rolled his eyes, sighed, and sort of slumped a bit in defeat; his hand twitched a little from remote withdrawal.

Steel Magnolias, and perhaps we could watch it after the end of *Love Story,* sort of a fun double feature. I know this wasn't the nicest thing to do, but it was his action movies that taught me that sometimes you needed to pull out the big guns in order to achieve a satisfactory ending.

My thinly veiled threat worked, and I could almost see the cogs kicking into high gear. I turned up the volume again so I could hear Jenny and Oliver's vows as they got married and to give him some more time. Right afterward he leapt up off the sofa and pointed toward the TV and shouted, "That's it . . . my answer . . . there . . . right there," giving me more proof that women were truly a more evolved life-form than men, which is evidenced by the fact that whenever men get excited they always lapse back into monosyllabic cave-speak. It was my turn to shrug.

He then told me that their vows summed up everything. Hers was long and his was short. I gave him a you're-gonna-have-to-do-better-than-that look, motioning for him to continue. He tried again and said that her vow was long and flowery (translation: poetic) and his was short and not so flowery (translation: direct and straightforward), but that it was obvious they both loved each other the same amount. He sat back down and grabbed for the remote control again. I held it above my head out of his reach and decided that now might be the time for me actually to read the *Men Are from Mars* book because I had no clue what he was trying to tell me. I wondered if *he* knew what he was talking about.

Now he was getting frustrated with me and told me that his point was that men and women were different, and the fact that I knew every line to *The Big Chill* and *Thelma and Louise* was the exact same thing as his knowing every special effect and grunt from one of his action movies. I nodded my head at this because he did seem to have a point, but surely that couldn't be it—it was much too simple. Reading my mind (a once-a-year occurrence), he told me that sometimes life was simple and that, in fact, he was a simple sort of guy. He explained to me that there didn't always have to be some terribly complicated emotional reason for every little thing he did. He told me that he simply liked guns, exploding buildings, car chases, and when the good guy wins. His next comment showed me that simple was a far cry from stupid, and that perhaps he understood me, and all women, a bit more than I gave him credit for. He said perhaps another reason he didn't feel the need to watch *Love Story* again was because he was already living it with me. How cheesy! But who cared? It was the perfect ending to our own movie, *Love Story Kicks Butt,* since he got the remote and I got my sappy tear-shedding moment.

CHAPTER SEVEN

Until Death
Do Us Part

A TALE OF TWO PARTIES

Cosmas has decided that English majors are stuck up, and he told me this in a very definitive tone, the one he used when declaring absolutes and facts—the voice of one plus one equals two and that you cannot know the position and momentum of an object at the same time (Heisenberg uncertainty principle). We were walking home from a party thrown by an English major (Ph.D., Middle English poetry; freelancer for fashion magazines), who was married to an art historian (finishing Ph.D., Northern Renaissance; working on dissertation on Albrecht Dürer). I didn't respond right away, allowing him the extra thirty seconds he needed to remember that I, his loving wife, happened to be an English major (granted, it was almost ten years ago, but once an English major, always an English major). Twenty-four seconds later he said, "All of them except you, that is." I smiled in the dark, noting that tonight he was speedier than usual, his norm being at least a thirty-second delay when responding to anything not related to science.

He was the classic absentminded but brilliant science guy who was continually processing obscure

He was the classic absentminded but brilliant science guy.

physics equations or brainstorming through molecular biology models—things that will change the world (at least, that's what I liked to think), which caused him to be a bit slow on the uptake when it came to other stuff.

It was my older brother, John, who once asked me how I knew Cosmas was brilliant, like how could I really know when I hadn't taken even one science class in college. I told him that I was pretty much going on faith—that somehow I just knew it to be true and I didn't require any proof. My brother, ever logical and always up for a debate, was just about to tell me that there was no scientific basis whatsoever for faith, but I cut him off with an afterthought and said, "Well, it's sort of the same way that I always knew you were brilliant, too." He paused for a moment then quickly saw my point. (Men are so easy.) Then my brilliant brother proceeded to ask if he could borrow a bit of cash and we arranged for a Western Union transfer, I suggested "Einstein" as a password. Funny, he said, and I said that humor was all I had that could stack up to the two geniuses in my life. My brother had a much shorter time delay than Cosmas, and he needed only a millisecond to process my sarcasm and to give me a hmphhh of disapproval.

Okay, so the party was a little bit of a disaster, but it had been fun for the first ninety minutes or so, which was a lot more than I could say for the last party we had gone to. I shuddered as I remembered back to a housewarming party we had attended a few months ago that had been thrown by two doctor colleagues of Cosmas's (a second-year cardiology fellow who lives with a Ph.D. population geneticist). It was hands down the most boring party I had ever been to in my life. I was the only person in the room who did not have an advanced degree in medicine or science, which meant that I was the only person in the room who didn't laugh at the talking amoeba joke that someone told. I just stood around and smiled as the room filled with talk of cloning genes, isolating proteins, and the latest issue of *Nature*'s full-color double-page spread showing blood vessel formation in a mouse, a common housefly, and a human. (Did you know that humans, mice, and flies are all incredibly similar biologically, once you get right down to it? Me neither. Do you care? Me neither.)

So I was standing over by the food table watching everyone devour Mary Sunshine's famous party onion dip (she had been kind enough to give me a batch to bring)—just an Asian Vanna White who nodded, smiled, and said over and over again, "Yes, it is yummy, isn't it? Yes, it sure is homemade; even the sour cream is homemade. Nope, there's no Lipton onion soup mix in it at all." Then they'd ask for the recipe and I would say, "Actually, even I don't have it . . . my suburban legend neighbor made it for me to bring. What's a suburban legend? Oh, just a little joke, doesn't mean anything really; well, if you have to know, think of a southern fried Martha Stewart on crack"—blank stare—"I mean, think Martha Stewart on 2-beta-carbomethoxyl-3-beta-benoxytropane," Aahhhh, now they got it and they smiled. "No, really, I *don't* have the recipe, and yes, if I did, I would, too, share it." Sheesh, those science women were an aggressive lot, and it took all my willpower not to suggest to them that if they were really that interested, then they should throw a dab under a microscope and sequence its DNA.

There was a time when my standard method for relieving boredom at a party was to find the couple with the meanest, bitchiest, hen-pecking girlfriend and flirt with her boyfriend. Not a sweet thing to do, but it certainly helped to pass the time. At this party my target would have been the tall gangly mathematician whose snotty girlfriend with the bad hair had snorted, in a most unattractive way, when I said that I had gone to NYU and was an English major. She herself had gone to MIT undergrad and was currently at Harvard getting her Ph.D. in astro-uptightness, and she then informed me that her calculus whiz boyfriend had been a Rhodes scholar. Now, I could

I decided to take the dumb-blonde-even-though-I'm-a-brunette approach.

have gone two ways here: the first would have been to be polite and say, "My, my, my, a Rhodes scholar, how very impressive"; the second option, of course, would be to retaliate. (I may read poetry now and again, but I am no wimp.) So I decided to take the dumb-blonde-even-though-I'm-a-brunette approach and said in a voice that was two octaves higher, and much silkier than my usual voice, "Ooooh, I just love Rhode Island. It's really one of my favorite states. I've had some of the best sex of my life there." This was followed by a flip of my hair and a sly wink at the mathematician. This caused him to blush a bit and his girlfriend to snarl and drag him out of the kitchen. I looked around for them now, thinking we could go another round, but then I remembered that I was married and that such behavior was probably not that becoming in a wife. I checked my watch and frowned at the fact that only eighteen minutes had passed since we arrived. I sighed, knowing that it was going to be one long night.

Looking across the room, I saw Cosmas talking to a few other people, and I went over, slipped into the circle next to him, and grabbed his hand. I was just in time to catch the end of yet another joke: "Get it? The chromosome walked across the street to get to a new gene pool!" and then they all burst out laughing. This time I smiled and laughed along with the group. Then I quickly interjected with a lightbulb joke (How does a Harvard man change a lightbulb? By placing the bulb in the socket and standing still, as he thinks the whole world revolves around him.) Cosmas let out a chortle, but no one else cracked a smile (Harvard alumni classes of '88, '90, '92, and '97). Luckily someone broke out with the fact that the earth actually revolved in the wrong direction necessary to screw in a lightbulb. Suddenly everyone was smiling again, and they eagerly started chattering about whether or not the joke would work if you happened to be in a different solar system from ours. Once again I tried to join into the conversation, "Wouldn't you have to be a rocket scientist to know that?" And sure enough, Ted (class of '88) *was* a rocket scientist. This was when I excused myself to go the bathroom, checking my watch on the way—another five minutes had passed.

As I stared at my reflection in the mirror, I muttered that science people took themselves way too seriously. My joke was funny, maybe not as funny as talking amoebas or walking chromosomes, but it at least warranted a smile. I didn't know what to do; it was obvious that I was not really meshing with this crowd all that well. I wanted to leave, but it seemed as if Cosmas was having an okay time, and it probably wouldn't be fair if I dragged him home early. I decided to tough it out for another thirty minutes.

Ten minutes later I heard talk about starting a game of Mighty Molecular Formation, which involved one team drawing out the molecular formation of an elemental property and then the other team guessing what it was and having to give their response in the two-letter periodic-chart code. There were bonus points if you could name the two elements to the right and left of that particular square on the periodic chart. It was now time to leave. Cosmas was now sitting on the couch talking to the mathematician and his bitchy girlfriend, and I wondered how I could get him away without having to go over there. My confidence at the moment was a bit wobbly, and I didn't think I could handle another run-in with someone who could insult me without my understanding what she was saying. I slipped back into the bathroom, whipped out my mobile phone, and paged Cosmas with the code of

453-911. When I walked back into the room Cosmas's pager went off, which caused the whole room to grab for their own pagers (ha-ha, made them all look). Cosmas looked a little puzzled when he saw the number. I caught his attention and mouthed, "Check the code card." I was so excited that we finally had an opportunity where my secret pager code guide was going to be put to good use.

When Cosmas first got his pager, and after I discovered that it did not allow for Internet text messaging, I came up with a numeric code sheet of various phrases. For example, 411 meant he needed to call me as soon as possible because I needed some information; 007 meant that I needed rescuing from my current situation; 143 meant I love you; 555 meant we're out of Diet Coke and could he buy some on the way home. I started out with a list of ten, but of course I got a bit carried away and managed to fit more than a hundred different phrases on a little card the size of a credit card (the joys of four-point type), had it laminated, and put it in his wallet. He excused himself from his science buddies and went through his wallet until he found the card. He squinted as he scanned the sheet and finally found out that 453 meant "Let's Go Now" and then he checked the subset B code and saw that 911 meant urgent, emergency, or right now (duh). He looked over at me, and I gave him my best

I'm-dying, strangulated-face look and then I gave him my best pleading-begging face. He checked the card again, and thirty-seven seconds later he indicated that he had finally figured it all out. We quickly said our good-byes and left, right as the game was about to start.

I decided it wouldn't really be nice to bring up that party; Cosmas had actually had a pretty good time at it, and it wasn't his fault that I found science people as boring as dirt. It was just that they all seemed to have very little to talk about besides science. Cosmas had tried to explain that none of them had time to read books, see movies, or look over the newspaper. I pointed out that he was more than able to talk about things other than science, and he gave me this look and sweetly said that was only because he was married to me. He told me that if we weren't married, then he'd probably spend every waking minute at the lab himself, and that I was really lucky to have met him when I did.

I had met Cosmas during a summer when he was so incredibly burned out by med school that he had sort of snapped and decided to try life on the other side for a while. He had grown his hair long, started shopping at Barneys, and spent his nights at chichi bars as opposed to the library. I distinctly remembered telling my friends after I had met him that he was the most nongeeky physics major I had ever met. (And the award for best leading actor for the summer goes to . . .) We laugh about it nowadays as his sunglasses-wearing, Dolce & Gabbana days are long gone, and he has explained it by telling me how he is just like the Atlantic puffin, which changes its appearance dramatically during mating season in order to attract a female bird; once the male nabs a female, he reverts to his more normal color scheme.

I guess I, too, had been a bit burned out on my *New Yorker*-reading, latte-inhaling, so self-congratulatorily oh-so-culturally liberal set, and I found his non—liberal arts side to be refreshing. Believe it or not, there were days when it was a bit of a bore to debate which nominee should win the National Book Award; sometimes I couldn't have cared less about the latest exhibit at the Brooklyn Musuem; and, yes, I agreed that small arty independent films could sometimes be slow and boring. Cosmas introduced me to action movies—pointing out the nuances between a Jean-Claude Van Damme film versus one starring Steven Segal, the beautiful choreography of the double-fisted gun-shooting violence of John Woo movies, and the detailed breakdown of why the big fight scene in the movie *Heat* was as close to perfection as you could get.

Believe it or not, there were days when it was a bit of a bore to debate which nominee should win the National Book Award.

I also fell in love with his deep passion for science, the way his eyes light up when his new issue of *Cell* magazine arrives each month (equivalent to the thrill of the September issue of *Vogue*). I knew it was true love when it didn't even faze me that he hadn't read even one book in the past year, and that when he did want to read a book it was always a mass-market thriller. But . . . I will admit that I was truly shocked, and a bit dismayed, when it came out at the party that he had never read *The Catcher in the Rye*.

We were chatting with an English major who now worked in advertising and her boyfriend who worked in the editorial department of the *Atlantic Monthly*. The three of us were all weighing in with our opinions on this year's winners of the Booker Prize (Cosmas was nodding his head in agreement with all of us), when Kenneth leaned in and whispered that the magazine's next big cover story was going to be some recently discovered letters between J. D. Salinger and his daughter, which caused us all to chime in with our disgust regarding the tell-all book that said daughter had written about him a few years back. So Cosmas said, "When did he die again?" Kenneth innocently asked, "When did who die?" I was trying to give Cosmas my best warning look to drop the subject—my eyebrows arching wildly. But alas, remember that damned thirty-second delay—it was sort of like watching a train wreck. It was actually worse than I feared it would be. Not only did he repeat "When did Salinger die?" but he followed with, "You know, I really feel I should read that book of his, what's it called, something Rye, *Fields of Rye*? . . . speaking of rye, did you know that they just finished the DNA sequence for rice, they're doing wheat next, and I believe, if memory serves me, that rye is third . . . isn't that interesting? . . ." Poor darling didn't even notice that Kenneth and his girlfriend, Jane, had basically stopped breathing and that my eyebrows had shot off my face and were now lying on the floor twitching like dying birds. I wasn't the only dumb brunette in the family.

Jane was gracious enough to say, "Jenny, your husband is just as funny as you are, what a jokester, *Fields of Rye,* so cute. I'll have to remember that one. . . ." But Kenneth, finally able to breathe, sputtered out, "DO YOU MEAN TO TELL ME THAT YOU HAVE NEVER READ *CATCHER IN THE RYE* BY JEROME DAVID SALINGER? In retrospect, the fact that he used Salinger's full name was a little uncalled for and should have been the catalyst in making me come to Cosmas's defense sooner, but I was in a bit of shock myself because I was equally as flabbergasted by his revelation. By now, a few more people had turned to stare and listen; Kenneth's voice had carried above the din because at a party like this—when someone talked about Salinger—vibrant, very-much-alive Salinger—everyone listened.

I knew I had to do something, and I racked my brain to figure out what Schwarzenegger would do in this particular situation. Hmmm, let's see, I had no gun, no explosives, and few muscles—so it was pretty doubtful that I'd be able to kill off all the witnesses. There was nothing else to do—I lied my ass off.

I laughed loudly in this choked-hyena way and said, "Cosmas, you silly boy, of course you've read *Catcher in the Rye,* you probably just don't remember." Not remembering was bad, too, but it was more along the lines of involuntary manslaughter than first-degree murder.

He shook his head no, and said that he was assigned it for summer reading during high school but that was the year he was heavily into Dungeons and Dragons so he did little else. (PLEASE TELL ME HE DID NOT JUST SAY WHAT I THINK HE JUST SAID.) My eyes were now shut, and I was ready to throw my arms over my face; the impact was coming, and it wasn't going to be pretty.

Honestly, at this point I wasn't sure whether it was even worth trying to save him. When you try to rescue someone from quicksand, there is always a chance of your getting pulled down with him, but dammit, I loved the guy and if he went, then I guessed I was going, too.

Through clenched teeth I said, "Sweetie, perhaps you've gotten your summers mixed up, Holden Caufield, laughs like a madman? Don't these things ring a bell?" trying to draw out my words as long as possible, *surely* we had hit the thirty seconds by now.

Cosmas was on his second gin and tonic (one is his normal limit, but when he had asked the guy who was tending bar for a ginger ale, the guy thought he was joking—liberal arts people like their booze—and gave him another G&T), which meant his response time was even slower than usual.

Again he shook his head and said more firmly now, "No, I definitely didn't read it, but I read the Cliffs Notes, so I still got an A on the test."

You could have heard a pin drop the room was so completely silent; admitting his use of Cliffs Notes was his third strike (no English major would ever admit using them, and I wondered whether I was now going to be ostracized by association).

It was like a pack of wild coyotes going after a lame deer—led by a guy named Curtis who was the classic, holier-than-thou, I'm-sooooo-smart-and-I-never-read-any-contemporary-fiction-published-after-1965. "So, Cosmas, tell us what other classics you've never read. What about, hmmm, let's go with something easy—

To Kill a Mockingbird?" I saw a flicker of recognition in Cosmas's eyes, and I jumped in with, "You know, the famous book by Harper Lee," which would hopefully deter him from bringing up the movie version. It was then that I tossed in the fact that, growing up, Harper Lee had lived next door to Truman Capote and that the character Dil was based on him. A slight murmur went through the crowd; there were many who did not know this juicy little literary tidbit, and they were happily filing it away in the front of their memory so they could use it to impress at their next social gathering.

Who said you can't learn anything from an action movie? I noted that there were two exits, one through the kitchen and one out the front hall.

Ha-ha, who said you can't learn anything from an action movie—this move had given me a few precious seconds to analyze the room's layout. I noted that there were two exits, one through the kitchen and one out the front hall. The one through the hall was crowded, but the kitchen pathway was now empty since all the food had been devoured (Mary Sunshine's famous party onion dip strikes again—I made a mental note that she would certainly get due credit for her assistance in this matter).

Cosmas was now well aware that the fangs were out, so he only gave a shrug about whether or not he had read the book. I could tell that he hadn't and he was calculating a mathematical risk assessment of the likelihood of some-one quizzing him on it if he lied and claimed to have read it. The probability was quite high. These days, English majors were growing increasingly bitter with the dawning of the era of technology; science was now king; Bill Gates was the richest man in the world; and it was predicted that computerized sales data would be the death of the midlist literary book. Cosmas shook his head, no, he hadn't read it, but he said that he had heard many great things about it (ooooh, nice try, hon). Kenneth, now feeling quite bad about being responsible for this mess (Peace Corps in '92, so he was a do-gooder), tried his best to help. He said, "Cosmas, don't mind Curtis, he's always detested science types; his math SAT score kept him out of Harvard even though he had a perfect verbal score. So you obviously aren't interested in the classics; what book have you read recently? It's always nice to have a fresh perspective in the crowd." Kenneth's own scores in the math department were pretty feeble as well, and he obviously didn't stop to calculate that the probability was quite low that Cosmas had even read a book recently. I knew it was going to be up to me to get us both out of this jam, and I tried to think what Detective John McClane would do right about now. Yippee ki yay!?

Cosmas smiled and said that the last book he'd read was called *The Shallow Man,* and that it was about a guy who dated only models and called them Things. There were a few furrowed brows, and I piped in with "A guy named Felske wrote it; it was like *Vox* but with an intriguing undercurrent of Bret Easton Ellis. Michiko gave it a fair review, if I remember correctly." Everyone nodded, but Curtis just sneered and said, "Oh please, the fact that Ellis and McInerny are even accepted as literary fiction is insane, *Bright Lights, Big City* was rubbish."

"Why, Curtis, when did you read that book; I thought you didn't read any contemporary fiction after 1965 . . . or is that just what you say to impress the librarians?" He looked momentarily embarrassed, then he turned his nose up at me and faced Cosmas once again, which proved he was a coward, unwilling to fight fair with me.

Right then it struck me, I knew what I had to do. I gave an inward sigh, glanced over at the love of my life—the one who had never read *The Catcher in the Rye,* and said in a strong clear voice, "Curtis, it's obvious that Cosmas excels in math, but why not ask him about his verbal score on the SATs." I paused briefly and answered my own question, "If memory serves me correctly, I think it was pretty close to a perfect score, *and* (here goes nothing) I found this out when he beat me in Scrabble." There were audible gasps, as I had beaten at least three people in this very room, Curtis being one of them. I tried to keep a straight face, but the searing pain I felt by even having to admit that Cosmas beat me that one time (honeymoon, beginner's luck) was definitely comparable to the time Rambo had to pull an arrow out of his own torso, pour gunpowder into the wound, and then set it on fire to clean it out.

Even Cosmas looked at me in wonderment as his calculations showed that the likelihood of my *ever* admitting defeat in Scrabble was, to him, virtually nonexistent. Then he smiled because he knew I had done it to save him, and he mouthed "I love you" to me. I mouthed back "I love you, too." Here was our golden opportunity, with everyone now looking at Cosmas with something close to awe; I looked down at my watch and said, "Oh my God, I forgot that the A&E version of *Pride and Prejudice* is on tonight, and I didn't set the VCR, so we really must be going! Good-bye, all." At which point I grabbed Cosmas's hand and we hauled ass out the kitchen door.

Now that we were almost home, I had finally found my reply to his earlier statement, and I said "Yes, we English majors are a bit stuck up . . . but you have to admit, our parties are definitely more exciting."

He nodded, smiled, and said, "Yeah, about as exciting as a field of rye."

A HAPPILY-EVER-AFTER MOMENT

I think there should be special fairy tales written just for married people that begin where our best-loved fairy tales end. When you're young, it's hard to see past that next pivotal moment in your life—like your next visit from the tooth fairy or the end of the flavor in the piece of gum you are currently chewing, so it's easy to buy into this happily-ever-after stuff. So you think, great, life is very neat and tidy in picture books; the right guy gets the right girl, and all the bad guys fall down wells or get eaten, and then you get to be happy for the rest of your life. Not a bad gig, if you ask me, and can I have another stick of gum?

So then you grow up a bit, you get a little wiser, you date a few jerks, you learn more about life, and then you fixate on more grown-up pivotal moments: getting your next promotion, finding the perfect jeans that don't make your butt look too big and make your legs look long and skinny, deciding what to buy everyone for Christmas. Well, you don't read as many fairy tales as you once did, so you don't really think about the happily-ever-after stuff as often; in fact, on your bad days you scoff at fairy tales and the whole notion of happily ever after. What you soon find out is that you can never completely expel the notion. So you say fine, you believe in it, but it's really far back in the recesses of your mind.

Then you meet the love of your life, you get married, and you get a whole new set of pivotal moments to fixate on: buying your first house, your first puppy, and finding the perfect pair of jeans that don't make your butt look too big and make your legs look long and skinny. You wonder where the happily ever after is, meaning, is it still way off in the future or is it right now,

I think there should be special fairy tales written just for married people that begin where our best-loved fairy tales end.

have you walked off into the sunset to come out in a kitchen where you're digging around under the bottom of the sink looking for the silver polish, are you living the happily ever after right now?

I carefully thought back through our two years of marriage and tried to figure out whether we've had a quintessential happily-ever-after moment during all our good times and bad. And I wondered how many more happily-ever-after moments we'd have throughout the future of our marriage. I contemplated the idea of everything being relative and how all our good times compared to one another—some memories so strong and sharp it was as if we were bellowing with laughter just yesterday—and how all our bad times figured into making the good times better.

So I decided to go ask Cosmas what his opinion was on our future and the happily-ever-after stuff. I found him stretched out on the couch reading a science journal. (His second-favorite position, wink-wink.) So I did that pretend-cough thing to try to get his attention. He said "What" but didn't look away from his magazine. I coughed some more, and he said "What" a little louder, but he still didn't look at me. And then I said his name in that tone of voice reminiscent of nails on a chalkboard, and I stomped my foot. So he laid his magazine on his chest and gave me his undivided attention. He said, "Yes, dear?" in a teasing way, knowing very well that I hated when he did that poor-me-ingratiating-I-have-no-backbone-because-my-controlling-wife-has-it-under-lock-and-key husband voice. So I said, "Stop joking around, this is important." And he wondered whether it was important like I-just-found-a-really-cute-hairstyle-in-this-magazine-I'm-reading-and-do-you-think-it-would-look-good-on-me? Or important like there-is-this-spider-in-the-other-room-and-I-need-you-to-catch-it-and-take-it-outside.

He blinked in anticipation and even wiggled his toes to show his interest in his darling wife's important question. So I rolled my eyes and went and sat on his chest, pinning him down, and said, "I would like your opinion on our future and the pursuit of the mythic happily ever after."

He made gagging noises and let his tongue loll out of his mouth to show that he'd rather capture ten thousand spiders and drive them into the countryside to set them free rather than discuss my fixation of the moment.

So I sort of bounced about on his stomach until he said, "I can't breathe." And I gave him one more final bounce for good measure and then made him sit up so I could sit next to him, meanwhile his science magazine slipped to the floor.

I knew that these sorts of discussions were painful for him, how he shied away from such talk of grandiose ideas and poetic dreams. He was a guy. He was very grounded in reality. But we had now been married long enough for him to know when I was feeling emotional and earnest, so he knew to try to take my question seriously and respond accordingly.

He told me that happily ever after was like a prism (ugh, a science analogy) that absorbed light and yet reflected it at the same time. So I said, "Huh?" So he paused and tried to think of a different analogy, and then he said that happily ever after was like a disco ball (now we were getting somewhere) that was way above you on the dance floor and was all shimmery with the promise of happiness that was always just ahead of us. But that happily ever after was also the light, those dancing dots on the floor coming off the disco ball surrounding you and passing over you. These dots were the happily-ever-after moments that danced over you throughout your life. So happily ever after was when he volunteered to do the dishes, did them, and remembered to rinse out the sink, too. It was the end of any fight. It was when one of us was sick in bed and the other was heating up a bowl of soup in the kitchen. It was sitting on the couch reading the *Sunday Times* together for the thousandth Sunday in a row. It was his reading a science magazine on the couch with me in his arms.

He said that happily ever after was like a disco ball that was way above you on the dance floor and was all shimmery with the promise of happiness that was always just ahead of us.

As far as the future was concerned, he said that he had no set plans except to spend his life with me. He said that when he looked at the future for me, he saw me phasing through hundreds more things and my telling him all about it during dinner each night. He told me that he knew this English major who once told him that the future for her was every single moment of every single day and that her favorite expression was still carpe diem, even though she knew it's been a bit played out. He told me that as a science guy he was keenly aware of the uncertainty of the future (it has to do with physics and quantum space theory—really, don't ask) and that he wasn't worried as long as he knew I had his back and he had mine.

I had never heard him so poetic. I had never been at such a loss for words. I reached down to the floor, picked up his science magazine, and handed it to him. He opened it up, lay back down, and started to read, and I burrowed into the couch next to him and laid my cheek on his shoulder, happy ever after. That was our moment. This is our story.

ACKNOWLEDGMENTS

Like a great shoe sale, it's hard to know where to start, so I'll just put my head down and charge forward. Thanks to: My mom for all her many years of unconditional love and endless support. John, the king of older brothers—wise, witty, and the voice of reason in my life. My late father, Seung H. Lee, and my sister, Helen Yoon Lee, whom I think of and live for every day. Laura Clement, my touchstone in life and laughter—I couldn't ask for a better best friend. Stephanie Staal, for her never-ending support and enthusiasm and bazillion hours of good phone! Jackie Snyder, for being by my side in shopping as well as in our marathon sessions of analyzing the meaning of our so-called lives. Jenner Sullivan, my glamorous partner in crime for all things fun and wild. Phillip Kim, a prince among men who has never wavered in his loyalty and friendship. Victoria Grantham, the only person I know who's as hyper as I am, and the ultimate cheerleader through the whole process. Christina Ohly, my kindred New Yorker spirit, who made my move out of New York City a little less painful. And extra special thanks to the whole Giallourakis/Despo clan—Mom and Dad G., Stamie, Aris, Alexander, and Orry (the best nephews in the world), and darling Christina. Who knew I'd be so blessed to have such a wonderful new family! Big fat thanks to Anne King, Tom Becker, Ken Yanhs, Stephanie Hom, Susie Stonehouse, Ruta, all my New York friends, all my new Massachusetts friends, especially those on Wendell Street in Cambridge. A special thanks to Joan Jones and to Bryan Huddleston, who have been on my case for ten plus years to write a book.

I am indebted to the Hill and Barlow Agency and especially to Rob McQuilkin who is everything an agent should be—smart, funny, patient, encouraging, calm, editorially savvy, sassy, and, most of all, a good friend. I am in complete awe of Workman Publishing Company, which is everything a book publisher should be and much, much more. Jennifer Griffin, my fabulous editor, with her cajoling, dedication, and determination, helped me write the best book I possibly could.